the experience of GOD

an invitation to do theology

(Revised Edition)

DERMOT A. LANE

Paulist Press
New York/Mahwah, N.J.

This book was first published by Paulist Press in 1981. The revised edition was
first published in 2003 by Veritas Publications.

Veritas Publications
7 / 8 Lower Abbey Street
Dublin 1, Ireland
E-mail publications@veritas.ie
Website www.veritas.ie

Library of Congress Cataloging-in-Publication Data

Lane, Dermot A., 1941-
The experience of God : an invitation to do theology /
Dermot A. Lane.—Rev. ed.
p. cm.
Includes bibliographical references and index.
ISBN 0-8091-4379-8 (alk. paper)
1. Experience (Religion) 2. Revelation. 3. Faith. I. Title.
BR110.L29 2005
248.2—dc22

2005012214

This edition published by Paulist Press
997 Macarthur Boulevard
Mahwah, New Jersey 07430

www.paulistpress.com

Printed and bound in the
United States of America

Dedicated
To former students of
Mater Dei Institute of Education,
Holy Cross College, Dublin
St Michael's College, Vermont,
University of Dayton, Ohio
'co-workers in the truth' (3 Jn 1:8)

CONTENTS

PREFACE TO REVISED EDITION

I n the late 1970s and early 1980s the turn to experience became prominent in Catholic theology and this was part of the context in which *The Experience of God: An Invitation to Do Theology* was published in 1981. The appeal to experience in Catholic theology was a relatively recent phenomenon facilitated in part by the Second Vatican Council which used the language of experience and more generally by the turn to the subject which had taken place in European philosophy in the nineteenth and twentieth centuries. A striking expression of this new appeal to experience in Catholic Theology appeared in a short article by Gerard O'Collins on 'The Pope's Theology' in *The Tablet* 27 June 1992 in which he praises the use of experience by John-Paul II in his encyclicals. O'Collins points out: 'In the 60s fear still lingered on such language (of experience) could encourage irrational individualism in religious belief and practise'[1]

Prior to the Second Vatican Council Catholic theology was largely *a priori*, deductivist and non-historical. Since Vatican ll Catholic theology has become experiential, inductivist and historically-conscious.

This appeal to experience in theology was followed quickly by a turn to hermeneutics: the art of interpreting experiences in the past in the light of the present and of understanding the present in the light of past experiences. Around the time that hermeneutics came to the fore in European and North American theology an equally significant development was taking place in Latin America, namely the turn to praxis and the recognition that praxis is also an important source of theology.[2] Clearly a logical line of development exists in the movement from experience to praxis and for many (e.g. Terrence Tilley) religious practise is recognised as an important source of theology.

A further development in theology also took place in what is described as the turn to language. Once it became clear that all experience is interpreted experience, then a new appreciation of the importance of language was inevitable. It is language that gives rise to thought, empowers praxis and weaves a narrative. Indeed the linguistic turn recognises that language houses experience and is the bearer of experience and for some is the source of all experience.

One further development in theology prominent at present is what I would characterise as the turn to the imagination. An increasing number of theologians are recognising the key role of imagination in faith and theology (e.g. David Tracy, James P. Mackey, Michael Paul Gallagher).

At this stage the reader may well be saying to himself or herself: given the shift to experience, to hermeneutics, to praxis, to language, and to the imagination, why bother to reissue a book on the importance of experience? The answer to this very reasonable question is that the turn to experience has now come full circle within theology and there is at present a renewed discussion of the place of experience in theology in the light of these different but complimentary turns. Two recent books bear this out.

In 2002 Charles Taylor published *Varieties of Religion Today: William James Revisited*. In that book Taylor revisits the influential work of William James, especially his *Varieties of Religious Experience* which was first published over one hundred years ago in 1902. Taylor is sympathetically critical of William James.

'Sympathetically', in the sense that many of the issues raised by William James in 1902 are still around today: a concern for the nature of religious experience; a focus on the negative experiences of fear, evil and suffering; the need to critique the agnostic vetoes against religious faith. 'Critical', in the sense that Taylor finds James' treatment of religious experience far too individualistic, neglectful of the social dimension of experience, and disdainful of institutionalised religion.

On the positive side William James highlighted the importance of experience for religious belief. In addition James offers an important critique of the agnostic rules for seeking the truth and critiques their commonly held view at that time that 'it is wrong always, and everywhere, and for anyone, to believe anything upon insufficient evidence'.[3] According to Taylor, summarising James: 'there are some domains in which truths remain inaccessible unless we go at least halfway towards them'.[4] To quote James directly there are cases 'where a fact cannot come at all unless a preliminary faith exists in its coming'.[5] James' response to the agnostic vetoes are as relevant today as they were one hundred years ago.

On the negative side William James' understanding of experience is too narrow, and his approach to religion is far too individualistic and privatised, having little regard for community, tradition, and sacrament as found in institutionalised Christianity.

The questions that William James' book on the *Varieties of Religious Experience* threw up in the early part of the twentieth century are still to the fore one hundred years later: questions about the meaning of religious experience, about the relationship between personal experience and sacramental practice, about the ethics of belief and the reasonableness of religious faith, and about the relationship between the spiritual and the social.

A second example of the current interest in experience can be found in the recently published book *Theology at the Void: The Retrieval of Experience* by Thomas M. Kelly.[6] Kelly writes in the light of the ever increasing influence of post-modernity and the threat it poses to theology. Radical deconstruction, as found in some forms of post-modernity, leads to relativism and this in turn opens up the possibility that we are living our lives in a void on the edge of an abyss. The only way of addressing this disturbing possibility of being surrounded by a void is through the appeal to experience and in particular by giving greater attention to the details of human experience.

Kelly traces the modern turn to experience back to Friedrich Schleirmacher who connects experience with a feeling of absolute dependence that puts us in touch with God. Kelly then presents critiques of Schleimacher by Wayne Proudfoot and George Lindbeck – both of whom argue from different perspectives that all experiences are structured by language and beliefs. Kelly next turns to the work of George Steiner who stresses that it is language that mediates an encounter with the other in literature and art. The presence of the other in language is ultimately grounded in God as the guarantor of all meaning and presence according to Steiner. Kelly concludes this lengthy review of experience by analysising Karl Rahner's theology of experience. For Rahner a close relationship exists between experience and language: language clarifies experience and the original experience clarifies language.[7] In brief, a dialectical relationship exists between experience and language, and Rahner if pressed, according to Kelly, would give priority to experience.[8]

It is in the light of these two recent publications I feel that a revised edition of *The Experience of God: An Invitation to Do Theology* is justified. It is hoped this revised edition of *The Experience of God* will give students some of the basic tools to enter this debate about the centrality of experience in understanding the mystery of God. Most of all it is hoped that by attending to the dynamism of human experience it will emerge that God is not a projection, but a gracious Presence, not a human invention, but a Reality found in experience, not a human creation, but a discovery of the hidden Other who is always already there in life. In particular, the temptation to reduce the mystery of God to one more item, one more explanation, one more piece of meaning must be resolutely resisted; instead the gracious mystery of God is the still Centre of all that dances in the world of science and society holding them together in a chaotic unity.

This divine Presence is always, already there, ahead of us and only becomes available through the personal act of faith. This act of faith is possible only on the basis of trust – not a blind trust, as William James points out, but a trust that is prepared to respond to a summons that opens up a world that otherwise would remain unavailable and inaccessible.

Many theologians today talk about 'the interruption of experience' and by this they mean that life is constantly interrupted by new experiences, both negative and positive, which can be of profound religious significance. Think for a moment of the impact on life of the following experiences: illness, death, beauty, injustice, forgiveness, tragedy, and love which continually challenge the meaning of life. Equally there are the historical experiences of the Jewish holocaust, what has come to be known as '9/11/2001' in the US, and the scandals of sexual abuse in the Catholic Church – all of which, over and above the horrendous trauma and suffering inflicted upon individuals, also shake social confidence in corporate institutions. These experiences, both personal and corporate, dramatically interrupt the flow of life and cry out for interpretation. Clearly, human experience never stands still.

There is also a sense in which it is possible to talk about the experience of transcendence as something that is a part of life for some. However, it is also true to talk about the transcendence of experience for others and by this we mean that a lot of experience simply passes us by in its meaning. The density of what takes place in human experience requires quite time for reflection if it is to be fully recognised; such stillness, however, is increasingly scarce in our fast-moving, noisy post-modern world.

What is clear is that whatever way one talks about experience, and clearly there are many ways, it seems true to say at least that all experience is profoundly historical and that one of the best ways to get a handle on the historical dimension of experience is to draw up a narrative. However, when a narrative is put together we quickly realise that it is not only incomplete, but it also contains messianic and eschatological moments, moments of promise awaiting fulfilment. To lose contact with the historical flow of experience is to lose contact with the core of our humanity and identity and to do this is ultimately to lose contact with God.

In conclusion, I should point out I have not changed the structure or the content of the original edition of *The Experience of God*. I have, however, nuanced the argument and its expression. In particular, I have stressed a little more the presence of universal or cosmic revelation and the place of imagination within the process of interpretation. In addition, I have added at the end of each chapter questions for discussion and an updated select bibliography. Lastly I have inserted some diagrams to make the text more user-friendly. These changes have resulted in adding twenty-five pages to the 1981 edition of the book.

I am grateful to Maura Hyland, the Director of Veritas, who first suggested to me that a revised edition of *The Experience of God* should be undertaken. I also wish to express my thanks to Maura Mitchell who gave significant help with the diagrams and to Shirley Nicholson who helped patiently with the word processing of the text.

Dermot A. Lane
September 2003

Introduction

The question of God is the ultimate question of life; it is the single most important question facing men and women in the world today. All other questions in theology are subordinate to the question of God. Thus Langdon Gilkey states, and we agree with him:

> Without some answer to the God-question, all talk about Word and Sacrament, about Scripture and hermeneutics, about the covenant community of the Church, about a Christ who is Lord of our life and history, and about the eschatological interpretation of history as God's action, is vain and empty.[1]

The precise formulation of the question of God varies from one generation to another. It depends on a variety of influential factors: culture, history, science and the prevailing philosophical mood. It could be suggested that the formulation of the God-question is a matter ultimately of taste and temperament. One thing is clear in this regard: the taste and temperament of the twenty-first century is quite different to the taste and temperament of the Middle Ages or indeed the taste and temperament of modernity.

The question of God today is not a question about proving the existence or non-existence of a being we call 'God'. If it were simply a matter of proving the existence of God, then we could proceed to assemble the best proofs and present them to the world, and all would be well. This, of course is simply not the case. Fortunately for human beings the question of God is more compelling than mere proof. The problem with the proof approach is that it runs the risk of reducing God to the modal status of an object somewhat like a star or stone 'out there', not unlike the rock of Gibraltar, which is incapable of affecting the individual on the personal level. This armchair approach to God fails to do justice to the activity of God in the world and the restless searchings of the human spirit. Such a spectator-like approach has given rise to what some justifiably have called 'the outsider God' and others refer to as 'the monarchical God'. One ends up positing a God who is remote, impersonal, detached and indifferent to the plight of the person in the world.[2]

The question of God for us today in the twenty-first century, as distinct from any other century, is about the possibility of experiencing God in the world. Where do we experience God in this life? At what point(s) in human existence does the reality of God impinge on human experience? The mystery of God is not some kind of theorem to be proved; it is rather, an experience to be lived.

This does not mean that we can now dismiss the proofs for the existence of God. Instead, the proofs for the existence of God come at a later stage in the discussion about God. It is only after one has been touched in life by the experience of God that the proofs begin to assume importance. The proofs for the existence of God are really an elucidation and elaboration of the experience of God.

The overriding horizon of this book, therefore, is the experience of God. Chapter One analyses what is involved in the experience of God and tries to highlight the peculiar character of such an experience. It also draws up criteria for evaluating an experience of God.

To talk about the experience of God of necessity involves discussing the different ways that God comes to people in the world. The natural complement to an analysis of the experience of God is an examination of the nature of revelation. Chapter Two takes up the issue of revelation and shows how the revelation of God to individuals comes in and through human experience. Different theories of revelation are evaluated, and special attention is given to the new orientation provided by Vatican II on revelation.

The experience of the revelation of God requires the personal participation of the individual if that experience is to be understood in all its implications. Hence Chapter Three deals with the activity of faith. Revelation creates faith, and faith receives revelation. The personal response in faith to revelation is an essential element in the experience of God.

The experience of God is one of the burning issues in theology today. It has two distinct but closely related dimensions: the action of God in revelation and the response of the individual in faith to that divine action. This book brings together the unity and interplay that obtains between human experience, the revelation of God and the faith of humanity. These are some of the basic elements that make up fundamental theology, that part of theology which deals self-critically with its own foundations. Systematic theology presupposes the sureness of these foundations. Most differences and disagreements in theology go back to the underlying presuppositions that are the proper preserve of fundamental theology. This book does not pretend to present a worked-out fundamental theology. It does hope, however, to open up a constructive perspective on some of the central issues that belong to fundamental theology. In doing so it is intended to provide a critical foundation for faith in the revelation of God by appealing to the richness of human experience.

In many respects this book is an invitation to do theology in a new key: to explore the religious dimension of human experience, to discover in faith the reality of God as co-present in human experience, to situate the gracious revelation of God to the person within experience, to ground the activity of faith as a response to the experience of God and to live life more fully by participating passionately in the revelatory orientation of human experience. God comes to us in experience. We receive God in experience. We do not project, create or posit God in experience. Rather we find God, already there ahead of us, in human experience.

Theology, from beginning to end, is about the critical unpacking of the revelation of God that takes place in human experience through faith. This description of theology may seem a little different, at first sight, to the classical account of theology as 'faith seeking understanding' and 'understanding seeking faith'. However the faith that seeks to understand has always been seen as a gift given to the individual in revelation. Faith comes from revelation. That faith must be critically grounded. It is not enough to 'cry God and fall silent. Hot on the heels of faith comes theology. Theology is ... faith scrambling for respectability'.[3] Part of that respectability is derived from the appeal to experience. Without this felt relationship to human experience, faith in God is in danger of appearing abstract and empty. Indeed, at times the impression was given that theology dealt only with the abstract world of ideas and concepts. Theology, in truth, is about life, the experience of life in all its spiritual implications, especially those that point toward the presence of God at the centre of existence itself. This experience of God, of course, needs to be expressed in ideas and concepts that are understandable. Experience is the basis of understanding, and understanding gives rise to deeper experiences. A close unity exists between experience and understanding. In this sense there is no real conflict between the classical understanding of theology and the one proposed in this book. Theology is faith seeking understanding that is critically grounded in the experience of the revelation of God. The underlying thesis of this book is that our faith understanding of God must be critically informed by, based on, and received from human experience.

1

EXPERIENCE, GOD AND THEOLOGY

My ultimate purpose, in all that I have written, is but to say this one simple thing to my readers—whether they know it or not, whether they reflect on it or not, human beings are always and everywhere, in all times and places, oriented and directed to that ineffable mystery we call God (Karl Rahner)[1]

New experiences of God, shaped by already held beliefs, in turn will 'correct' one's previous interpretation of those beliefs and thereby enrich future possible experiences (Ormond Rush)[2]

One of the most significant developments in Christian theology in the twentieth century has been the recovery of experience as an integral element in the exercise of theology. This development is especially remarkable in Catholic theology in view of the fact that not so long ago there was something of a magisterial ban against the use of experience in theology. This distrust of the appeal to experience was brought about by the Modernist crisis at the beginning of the twentieth century. During that time a rather narrow, psychological and subjectivist understanding of experience was in existence. As a result the unfortunate impression was given that theology was simply an outgrowth of experience in this narrow sense. This outlook was condemned in 1907 by Pope Pius X in his encyclical *Pascendi Dominici Gregis*. By way of reaction against Modernism Catholic theology deliberately isolated itself from historical, social, scientific and cultural developments. Barriers were erected between life and theology. Something of a divorce took place between theory and practice. Grace and nature became exclusive opposites. The argument from authority assumed absolute significance. This kind of apartheid was inconsistent with the witness of the theological tradition and Christian living. It could not be followed through rigorously and therefore could not last for long. Gradually in the early 1940s and 1950s theology once again moved outwards towards the other sciences. Similarities as well as differences between theology and the other sciences emerged. Soon it became clear that theology was concerned not only with the passing on of Scripture and tradition, but also with some form of critical correlation between human experience and the Gospel of Jesus Christ.

Today most discussions about the nature of theology among Catholic theologians include reference somewhere along the line to the role of human experience. David Tracy argues convincingly that the principal sources of fundamental theology are 'the Christian fact and contemporary experience'.[3] Michael Schmaus points out that faith, which is the material object of theology, 'is impossible without some measure of understanding and experience'.[4] Karl Rahner asks provocatively: 'If Christianity is nothing other than the clear expression of what man experiences indistinctly in his actual being ... what reason could I have then not to be a Christian?'[5] Edward Schillebeeckx asserts that 'the world of human experience is the only access to the saving reality of revelation and faith ... How could we listen to a revelation from God, how could it be a revelation to man if it falls outside our experience?'[6] Bernard Lonergan holds that experience, 'especially repeated experience, of one's frailty or wickedness raises the question of one's salvation and, on a more fundamental level, there arises the question of God'.[7]

At the same time, these theologians are careful to point out that this relationship between theology and experience does not imply in any sense a reduction of theology to experience.[8]

Obviously a real difference exists between claiming that theology is related to human experience and holding that theology is simply an outgrowth of human experience. Perhaps even more significant is the way that the language of experience over the years has come back into official Church documents.[9] Pope John Paul II in his first encyclical, reminds us that the 'Church's fundamental function in every age and particularly in ours is to direct man's gaze, to point awareness and experience of the whole of humanity toward the mystery of God'.[10]

An equally strong concern about the importance of experience, though perhaps less remarkable from an historical point of view, also exists in Protestant theology. The legacies of Friedrich Schleiermacher and William James continue to be enjoyed and refined by modern Protestant theology. According to Paul Tillich: 'The question of experience ... has been central ... whenever the nature and method of theology have been discussed'.[11] He describes experience as 'the medium through which the sources of theology speak to us'.[12] For Tillich 'experience receives and does not produce' in theology.[13] Langdon Gilkey develops an impressive introduction to theology out of an analysis of human experience which enables him to conclude: 'All religious talk ... is talk about the ultimate and the sacred as it appears in ordinary experience'.[14] He constructs this introduction by uncovering a dimension of ultimacy in our secular experiences of contingency, relativity, temporality and autonomy.[15] John E. Smith argues persuasively that the disclosure of God to the world takes place in and through human experience.[16] For Smith, human experience is the key to understanding religious truth.[17]

This development in Catholic theology during the twentieth century, coupled with the centrality of experience in Protestant theology, calls for some discussion and clarification.

The appeal to experience has become so commonplace that it is now in danger of becoming vacuous. The word 'experience' is, to say the least, a rather slippery one. It can be made to mean just about anything one wishes it to mean. If experience is to become a genuine source of theology in the light of Scripture, tradition and the authority of the Christian community, then there is a pressing need for precision in the use we make of and the meaning we attach to experience. What do we mean by the appeal to experience in theology? Is such an appeal to experience in danger of becoming a subjective cloak or even worse a new smokescreen against critical reflection? The purpose of this opening chapter is to clarify the meaning of the word 'experience', to explore the different kinds of experience that are possible in life, to examine the peculiar character of religious experience, to discuss the relationship that exists between experience and doctrine, and to suggest some basic criteria for evaluating religious experiences. It is hoped that a treatment of these issues will throw a little critical light on the use we make of experience in theology and perhaps advance the way forward toward some ecumenical agreement on how Christian theology is done as well as providing a point of departure for interreligious dialogue. In this way we will be laying the critical foundations for a theology, in subsequent chapters, of the interplay that exists between revelation and faith in experience.

The Meaning of Experience
We can begin our exploration of the meaning of experience by excluding at the outset the more obviously deficient uses of the word.[18] For some, experience is synonymous with reference to a form of subjective emotionalism. Here experience is reduced to the level of euphoric outbursts of transient emotions. Such phenomena may be the result of a passing psychological mood or they may be induced by artificial external stimuli. In either case we are dealing with a situation that is temporary, superficial and unrepresentative of the normal human condition. To this extent such experiences cannot be regarded as reliable channels of human understanding. Others restrict the word 'experience' to the passive reception of sense-data out there. Here experience is confined exclusively to a direct contact with the empirically given world. This empiricist view of experience must also be rejected because of the large areas of life that are automatically excluded. A third and not untypical view of experience is one which says that language determines the character of all human experience. Not only is language descriptive of human experience, but it is also prescriptive of human experience. The language we use in life

determines the kind of experiences we have of the world around us.[19] This particular outlook, even though it does contain some truth, must also be put aside at this stage because it ignores the spontaneity of experience and the drive inherent in such experiences for new expression. These restrictive accounts of experiences alert us to some of the more obvious pitfalls that are around when trying to work out a critical theology of experience. What then are the basic ingredients of a human experience? Experience involves first and foremost a human subject and reality. By a human subject we mean an individual self that is capable of seeing, feeling, thinking and discerning. The element of feeling, as distinct from emotion, is important in the life of the human subject. On the other hand the word 'reality' embraces the external world as composed of spirit and matter in which the subject lives. Following on this there must be some form of conscious encounter between the subject and reality if there is to be any genuine experience. The word 'encounter' suggests a degree of contact between the subject and the world. It implies that within experience we find something already there; we come up against reality as given, and therefore prior to us. We confront persons and events in the world and we do so in such a way that we receive whatever it is that we encounter without being responsible for producing what we receive. Encounter, however, is only the beginning of experience since within encounter we do not move beyond the surface of reality. Reality has more to it than surfaces; it also has depth and breadth.

Moving from encounter we must go on to posit a process of interaction between the subject and reality. It is through this process of interaction that experience begins to actualise itself as event in the life of the subject. The interaction is composed of a chain of events. These include a response or reaction from the subject, as conscious subject, toward reality. Following on this, reality is refracted or broken back upon the subject. This in turn evokes a process of critical reflection in the subject.

Experience, therefore, is the outcome of the interaction that takes place between the subject and reality. Experience should not be located as something simply within the subject who looks at life but rather as the outcome resulting from critical interaction between the subject and reality. This qualification excludes the reduction of experience to what Heidegger once called the mere 'gawking' at objects lying 'out there'. Experience is a more complex process; it is the critical assessment of reality by the subject through the movements of response, refraction and critical reflection. Within experience there is always a reciprocal flow between the subject and reality which creates a new relationship, a new level of personal participation, a deepened form of awareness and understanding in the life of the individual. Thus experience is never merely subjective or objective. Such is a false antithesis. It is, instead, that which emerges out of a living relationship between the subject and reality.

A basic characteristic of experience is that no one experience discloses the totality of reality. Repeated experiences, no matter how contrasting, are a necessary component in the process of understanding reality. A succession of similar experiences can have a cumulative effect on human understanding. A certain pattern may emerge within experience, and this, in turn, can give rise to insight and new understanding. Past experiences affect present experiences and present experiences influence future experiences. Every experience exercises a critical function in relation to other experiences. This holds true as a basic principle in regard to both one's own experiences and the experience of others.

An important factor in any theory of experience is the role that the community plays. This role is two fold. On the one hand the community provides the overall horizon of understanding within which human experiences begins to make sense. There can be no such thing as a 'pure' experience without reference to some elements of understanding. Experience without understanding is an empty event. T. S. Eliot points out this danger in the following way; 'We had the experience but missed the meaning'.[20]

A real distinction does in fact exist between having an experience and knowing that you are having an experience. The essential element of understanding that is brought to bear on human experience is usually the inherited wisdom of the community we live in and the tradition we have been brought up in. Prior to experience this horizon of understanding, derived from the community, exists in a pre-critical and pre-reflective form.[21] After experience and in the light of multiple experiences the individual critically and reflectively appropriates the horizon of understanding belonging to his or her community. This transition from a pre-critical to a post-critical level of understanding is essential to the growth of the individual in the life of the community. In fact it is only through different experiences that the emergence of an individualised self-consciousness and personal identity takes place. We do not come into the world with a ready-made self. Rather we enter life with a capacity to become which is shaped by our experiences of reality. We leave the world with a constituted self shaped by the experiences we have undergone. The self develops out of experiences with reality, especially the reality of the human community composed of other selves.

On the other hand, having undergone this movement from a pre-critical to a post-critical level of understanding, the individual is still dependent on the collective wisdom of the community. Individual experiences must be tried and tested against the corporate experiences of the community. In most cases the community acts as a guide for understanding the significance of human experience. This does not mean that individuals are necessarily tied to the wisdom of any one particular community. They are always free to move beyond or outside the community to which they originally belonged. If they do this, however, they must move into some other community which will act as norm to their experiences. Individuals as individuals cannot critically assess their own experiences without reference to some other group or community. To do otherwise would be to run the risk of arbitrary subjectivism.[22] The very nature of experience as something which is simultaneously subjective and objective requires that the experiencing subject be in touch with some living community.

It should be noted, at this stage, that experience usually contains more than we can fully express or clearly articulate. The interpretation of experience usually falls short of the full content of the experience in question. Often we will return to the same experience from a slightly different angle in an attempt to grasp more of its full significance. And yet the totality of an experience is always greater than the sum of its individual parts. The implications of an experience can take time to unfold, and it may happen that the real significance of an experience only emerges at a later stage in the life of an individual.

These preliminary remarks about the meaning of experience apply to all human experiences whether one is talking about science or philosophy or theology. Clearly experience within this framework is a uniquely formative element. Furthermore, experience is the basic source of all human understanding, including religious understanding. In summary, the individual is what he or she experiences, and 'things are what they are experienced as'.[23] In the words of Henry James:

> Experience is never limited, and it is never complete; it is an immense sensibility, a kind of huge spider web of the finest silken threads suspended in the chamber of consciousness, and catching every airborne article in its tissue. It is the very atmosphere of the mind.[24]

It is against this background on the meaning of experience that we can now distinguish the existence of the different kinds of experiences.

A Classification of Different Kinds of Human Experience

Obviously the individual is capable of undergoing a wide variety of human experiences in life. Broadly speaking these experiences may be divided into primary and secondary experiences, or what are sometimes called ordinary and extraordinary experiences,[25] or what others refer to as outer and inner experiences.[26] Perhaps the clearest classification is simply that of sense-experience and depth-experience.

Ordinary experiences may be described as those everyday subject-object encounters we have in life. These experiences are primarily sense experiences and do not go beyond the external surface of life. Such experiences cover the coming and going of everyday activity. However, in addition to this external sense contact with the world, there are those special moments when we go below the surface of life to discover a deeper dimension which is not immediately evident. These extraordinary experiences disclose the existence of a 'depth dimension' in human existence.[27]

This 'depth dimension' in life is the point where we discover such diverse realities as meaning, value, goodness, beauty, and truth. The discovery of these realities is made through the mediation of an ordinary human experience. As such the discovery is always indirect. We do not experience truth as an object like an apple hanging from a tree.

Bernard Lonergan distinguishes between the world of immediate experience and the world mediated by meaning.[28] The world of immediate experience is the world in which the child moves and lives; it is the given world composed of the everyday sense data of seeing, touching and hearing. In contrast, the world mediated by meaning is the world of the adult; it is the world intended by questions, organised by intelligence, described by imagination and language, and enriched by tradition. The movement by the individual from the world of immediate experience to the world mediated by meaning brings about a change in the life of the subject. Lonergan likens the transition from one world into the other world to the move by Plato's prisoners from the cave composed of dark images to the universe of light and brightness.[29] The change requires a real adjustment in the life of the individual. For one thing it alters the quality of self-consciousness. In addition it opens up the invisible presence of a whole new world of meaning. The world of meaning is not immediately or directly available to the individual. This does not mean that this world is less real. If anything it seems to suggest that 'the really real' world is the world that lies both within and at the same time beyond the everyday world given in immediate ordinary experience. This movement by the subject from a world of objects out there into a world mediated by meaning opens up new horizons of human understanding.

It is within the realm of this new world of meaning generated by secondary, depth-experience that we can begin to talk about what is involved in a religious experience. The underlying characteristic of a religious experience is that individuals find themselves called and drawn into a new relationship with that which is variously termed the Transcendent Other, the Holy, and the Ultimate. From a structural point of view a religious experience follows the same pattern as that of a secondary depth-

　　　　THE EXPERIENCE OF GOD

experience. A disclosure is made through the medium of a human experience. This disclosure is identified with what is called the religious dimension of life. To this extent every religious experience is always a depth-experience, though not every depth-experience is necessarily a religious experience. As a basic principle we can say that a religious experience is at one and the same time an experience of something else.[30] It is this experience of 'something else' which serves as the medium disclosing that dimension in life which is called religious. A more accurate way, therefore, of talking about religious experience would be to refer to the 'religious dimension of human experience'. In practice, however, this expression is often abbreviated into 'religious experience'.[31] To put this in more traditional terms we might say that every religious experience is a sacramental experience. This account of the different kinds of human experience may be summarised diagrammatically as follow:

DIFFERENT KINDS OF EXPERIENCE

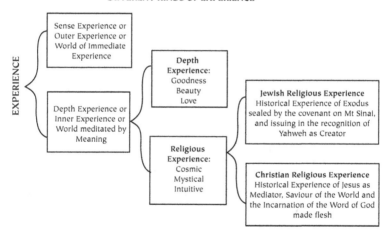

The Peculiar Character of Religious Experience

The whole area of the religious dimension of human experience came to the fore in theological discussion in the latter half of the twentieth century.[32] There is little doubt that the centre of gravity in religion has shifted from authority to experience. Some will see this as a slight on authority. Others will see it as an opportunity for authority to assume a new credibility and stylus. In fact, the more emphasis that is placed on religious experience the greater the need for some form of authority to act as a guide and interpreter of the multiple experiences that people undergo. Authority must address itself to present experience as well as conserving traditions about past experiences. The real issue facing authority and believers alike is the peculiar character of religious experience. What happens when we encounter the religious dimension of human experience? What should we expect from a religious experience? Are religious experiences a fairly frequent occurrence, or are they something rare and exceptional?

Again, somewhat like the notion of experience itself, certain misunderstandings must be removed about the nature of religious experience. One of the most common misunderstandings is the suggestion that some kind of direct and immediate contact with the sacred takes place in religious experience. This outlook is based first of all on a mistaken view of the nature of experience itself. As already seen, the notion of experience, especially at the level of depth-experience, is a little more intricate than one of direct vision. A movement by the subject takes place, which brings that subject beyond the visible frontiers of the empirical world into a new invisible world mediated by meaning and depth.

A more serious difficulty arises, however, from this distorted view of religious experience. It is the implication that God is directly available to some people and/or that some people have direct access to God. These particular implications, however ill-conceived, take us into the very heart of most questions about the religious dimension of human experience.

It must be pointed out clearly that from the side of the human person it is extremely unlikely that the individual could sustain direct contact with God in this life. It has always been held, with justification, that we must first of all receive the grace of 'the light of glory' in order to enter into the beatific vision with God. The purpose of 'the light of glory' is to raise the individual up to a new level and capacity so as to be able to sustain the vision of God. Furthermore, St Paul reminds us vividly that in this life we see dimly as in a mirror, but then we shall see him face to face.[33] In addition we learn from St Thomas that whatever we know and experience is determined by our native capacity (finite and limited) to know and experience.[34] These basic principles suggest that all human experiences of God are indirect, being mediated through our experience of creation[35] and the revelation of God in Jesus. This suggestion is borne out by the Jewish and Christian traditions which hold that no one has seen God and lived.[36] We must avoid, therefore, giving the impression that humanity has direct access to God.

From the side of God, we must be less assertive about the nature of religious experience. Obviously we cannot place limits on the action of God's self-communication to the individual in the world. Every religious experience is always a grace given by God to the person. Religious experience is never simply the result of human effort. If anything, it would appear that God comes to us at times and in ways we least expect. The grace of God in the world, which comes to us through experience, more often than not disturbs us with its demands or surprises us with joy through its richness. Yet it must be remembered that God in the normal course of events and especially in the history of salvation addresses the person in the human condition. Grace grows from within nature; it does not bypass or destroy nature. The history of God's saving contact with people is one of gracious mediation through the experience of creation, history, the incarnation, and the sacramental system of the Church.

Having challenged the view which says that religious experience involves ' immediate' contact with God, we must also avoid the other extreme which holds that God is simply mediated through human experience. This could give the equally false impression that God is not experienced from the outset but is only inferred logically from something else. In this case God would arrive as some kind of third term subsequent to experience and, then, rather late and as some kind of stranger.[37] In effect contact with God is severed because God appears to exist outside the pale of human experience. In the end God becomes a construct derived from the intramental activity of the subject.[38]

The question of religious experience is a little more complex. We must go beyond the alternatives of 'immediate' and 'mediate'

---

experience of God. Instead, we wish to suggest that God is co-experienced and co-known through the different experiences and knowledge of the human subject. God is co-present to us from the outset in all our experiences.[39] With Aquinas we want to hold that God is known implicitly in everything that is known.[40] Religious experience enables us to see that which was already there in our experience but which we failed to acknowledge explicitly in the first instance. As already noted, a religious experience is always an experience of something else at one and the same time. It is an experience which involves the subject in the dynamic activity of co-experiencing, co-knowing and co-discovering God in the world. Thus Rahner can say:

> The tendency today to talk not about God, but about one's neighbour, and to use not the term 'God' but 'world' and 'responsibility for the world' – has an absolutely solid foundation.[41]

This tendency has a solid foundation because we do not experience God *in se* apart from our neighbour and the world. Rather we co-experience and co-know God in our experience and knowledge of the neighbour and the world. In the suggestive words of Schillebeeckx. 'God is the transcendent third in all our human experiences and above all in our interpersonal relationships'.[42]

Another way of putting this is to say that while God is immediately present to the subject in the world it is necessary for this immediacy of God to be mediated through human experience. Thus many theologians today talk about the 'mediated immediacy' of God to the human person.[43] This immediacy of God is reminiscent of the God of Augustine who is more intimate to the soul than the soul is to itself. If we did not already sense God implicitly in our experiences we could not even begin to raise the question of God. When we do find God explicitly in our experiences we are recognising a presence that was always there. It was this kind of theological position that prompted Pascal's remark: 'Take comfort; you would not be seeking me if you had not already found me'.[44] Carl Jung makes a similar point in his reference to a notice outside a retreat house in Switzerland which says 'Whether called upon or not God will be present'. The same perspective is found in T. S. Eliot:

> We shall not cease from exploration,
> and the end of all our exploring will be to arrive
> where we started,
> and know the place for the first time.[45]

In other words God is immediately present to us in the order of being (*ordo essendi*) and mediately present to us in the order of human knowing (*ordo congnoscendi*). While it is true to say that the divine order of being is ontologically prior to the individual, it must also be recognised that it is logically subsequent to – or better concomitant with – human experience and knowledge. The central point here is that the co-presence of God in the world communicated through the religious dimension of human experience, is neither a presence directly available only to a privileged few nor a presence mediated simply through logical deduction to the learned. Instead the reality of God in the world is a presence that is accessible to all; it is a gracious omnipresence in which every human being 'lives, moves and has her or his being'[46] whether it is consciously recognised or not. One of the primary tasks of theology today is to 'unpack' our human experience of this omnipresent God. The real issue is how to make the individual experientially co-present to God. The question of God is not about the absence of God to the person; it is about the absence of the person to God who is permanently co-present. In this context, we must remember that the experience of God is not the experience of another object out there which we see only if we look hard enough and long enough. Rahner reminds us umambiguosly:

> For that God really does not exist who operates and functions as an individual existent alongside of other existents, and who would thus as it were be a member of the larger household of all reality. Anyone in search of such

a God is searching for a false God. Both atheism and a more naive form of theism labour under the same false notion of God, only the former denies it while the latter believes that it can make sense out of it.[47]

When we talk about an experience of God we are talking about an experience that sustains and deepens and borders and surpasses all other human experiences. Thus theologians, in an effort to overcome simplistic objectifications of the divine, talk about God as 'the ground of being and the depth of human existence' (Tillich), 'the whither and term of human transcendence' (Rahner), 'the beyond in our midst' (Bonhoeffer), and 'the divine Thou glimpsed in the I-thou encounter' (Buber). The experience of the religious dimension of life, therefore, is a particular configuration of human experience that enables us to see within and beyond the visible world at one and the same time. As such, religious experience has a strongly intentional character about it; it is directed toward a reality which is other than and prior to the perceiving subject. And yet religious experience is always a graced experience; it is not chosen but given, not created but received, not fabricated but found.[48]

At this stage the inevitable question will arise as to where does one fit mystical experience into the above scheme. The category of mystical experience is notoriously difficult to tie down. For most people it means some kind of direct and intimate union with the presence of God. The obvious temptation is to dismiss this type of religious outlook as somewhat fanciful. However, a certain caution is called for here. It is at least possible that the individual, after undergoing many rich religious experiences, might momentarily disregard the medium disclosing the religious dimension of life and thus focus, though darkly, on the transcendent. Such is conceivable in the lives of those who are particularly advanced and matured in the ways of God. This form of personal and direct union with the presence of God, however, is difficult to maintain for any length of time. It is a special grace for which there would appear to be some evidence in the history of spirituality and which, therefore, cannot be excluded. As a possibility it acts as a useful corrective

THE EXPERIENCE OF GOD

to those who concentrate too much on the medium in religious experience to the neglect of personal communion with the transcendent reality of God which is the goal of all religious experience.[49] This can happen in theology when doctrine and belief become an end in themselves rather than a means of penetrating the incomprehensible mystery of God. However, mystical experience should not be presented as the primary or principal experiential point of contact with God. Rather it is a possibility subsequent upon many and various other religious experiences. Further, mystical experience is more the exception when one is talking about the gracious action of God in the world. It should be noted in this regard that most mystics warn that such experiences are only valid for and recognisable by those who have already undergone the experience. They are not the norm for those setting out in search of God. In brief, the difference between religious experience and mystical experience is a difference of degree and not of kind.

An example or two may help to illustrate the above perspective on religious experience. A human being may be immediately present to us, say in a bus, without our recognition of that individual as uniquely personal. However, when we begin to experience certain signs and gestures from that individual we may also begin to co-experience the immediacy of the person to us. The signs and gestures are not the person, but they are an essential element in our experience of that individual as unique and personal. In a similar way, when we begin to experience the world in all its diverse activity, we begin to co-experience God not so much as something seen in the world, but as the basis of all seeing, not as an object known in the world, but as the basis of all knowing, not as a thing of value but as the source of all value, not as a particular meaning, but as the ultimate context in which all meanings subsist, not as a being, but the origin of all being.[50]

This particular analogy of interpersonal experience can be further explored as a useful way for understanding the relationship between God and the world as disclosed in religious experience. We can say, with Aquinas, that God stands in relation to the world in a way that reflects the relation of the soul to the body.[51] It is only in and through our experience of the bodily activity of another human being that we can begin to discover the existence of that dynamic transcendent reality we call a person. Equally, it is only in and through our experiences of the rhythm of life in the world that we can discover God as that transcendent reality who is immanently present to the world. This does not mean that we identify God in any way with the world any more than we would identify a human person with his or her body considered merely as physical. The analogy, of course, like any good analogy, has its obvious limitations. For instance the person is dependent on the body in a way that God is not dependent on the world.[52]

Another example that illustrates the dynamics of a religious experience could be taken from the field of artistic experience. When we experience a work of art we are initially confronted with surfaces that arrest our attention. These surfaces at the same time draw us into a depth of meaning which is not immediately evident. Clearly, within the artistic experience there is more than surface, and yet surface is the point where depth begins to insinuate itself upon us and so become co-present to us. Too often in the artistic experience, and indeed in religious experience, we try to bypass the surface and go directly to the depth. When this happens the depth dimension of both art and religion is severed from experience and thereby distorted.[53] Today the emphasis in religion is being placed upon experience with a view to rediscovering the depth dimension of existence itself. While the artistic experience does contain some useful parallels, at the level of structure, with religious experience, there is, as we shall presently see, a real difference in tone and character between the two experiences.

A final example to bring out the unique character of religious experience (the co-presence of God in human experience) is the image of the sun's presence in the act of seeing. God is present to the individual in experience in a way that is analogous to the presence of the sun in the act of seeing. The sun provides light in and through which we see; even though we do not see the sun directly we nonetheless participate in the light of the sun. In a similar though limited way we can say God is present in our deepest experience of existence; even though we do not see God directly we nonetheless participate in the omnipresence of God in such experiences.[54] This section on the peculiar character of religious experience could be summed up in the following way:

> God is co-experienced and co-known,
> co-present and co-active,
> in the interruptions of human experience,
> in the drive towards self-transcendence,
> in dynamic intentionality of the subject,
> in the sting of contingency,
> in the quest for meaning,
> in 'the search for truth, the insatiable need for the good, hunger for freedom, nostalgia for the beautiful and the voice of conscience'.[55]

The following three diagrams (pp.34-35) seek to capture, however inadequately, the dynamic and peculiar character of religious experience.

Religious Experience and/or Doctrine

Because religious experience has become so important and central in the lives of many people there is now a real danger of playing down the role of doctrine in theology. Indeed some would try to suggest that doctrine is secondary in comparison to religious experience. This outlook springs from the false premise that there is such a thing as a chemically pure religious experience. The idea of a 'neat', uninterpreted experience in religion is a wishful projection that should be discouraged. We have already seen that experience always presupposes some degree of understanding. Every experience of God is influenced by some element of religious knowledge and background. People are never entirely free from theories and belief systems. Experience always belongs to someone who exists as a subject at a particular time in a particular place with a particular value system. Each one of these elements shapes and influences the religious experience of the subject. Not only that, but without some background of religious knowledge and doctrine there would be no religious experience. Doctrine and beliefs are essential to religious experience. They supply the basic horizon of understanding within which religious

THE PECULIAR CHARACTER OF THE EXPERIENCE OF GOD

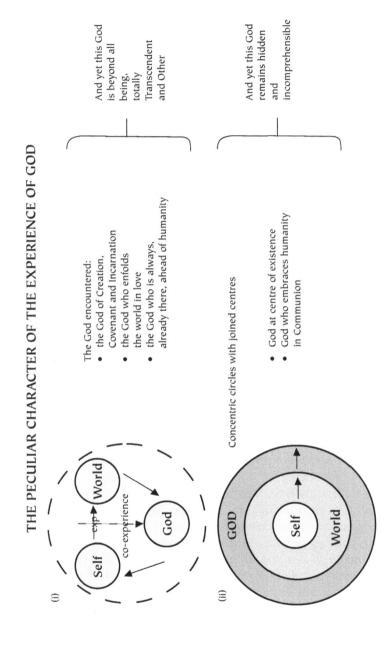

(i)

The God encountered:
- the God of Creation, Covenant and Incarnation
- the God who enfolds the world in love
- the God who is always, already there, ahead of humanity

And yet this God is beyond all being, totally Transcendent and Other

(ii)

Concentric circles with joined centres

- God at centre of existence
- God who embraces humanity in Communion

And yet this God remains hidden and incomprehensible

THE PECULIAR CHARACTER OF THE EXPERIENCE OF GOD

(iii)

An ever deepening spiral
with the mystery of God
at the centre
of the self and the world

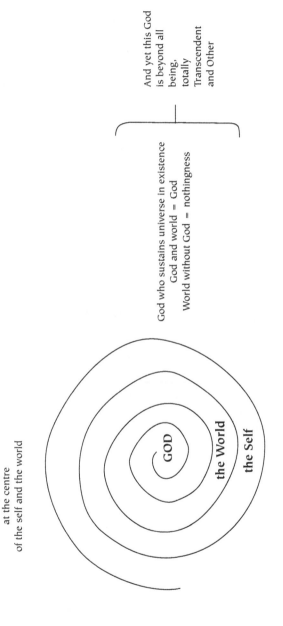

the World

the Self

GOD

God who sustains universe in existence
God and world = God
World without God = nothingness

And yet this God
is beyond all
being,
totally
Transcendent
and Other

experience occurs.[56] Most of all, doctrines provide us with a religious interpretation of experience.

On the other hand, doctrine for the sake of doctrine without reference to experience runs the risk of becoming 'a noisy gong or a clanging cymbal'. It is hardly an exaggeration to say that a serious rift occurred between experience and doctrine in Catholic theology during the first half of the twentieth century which is only now being restored.[57] It is this rift that has brought about a disenchantment among some with certain aspects of Church doctrine today. If doctrine is not related to human experience it will inevitably become marginal in the lives of believers. Further, doctrine must be able to evoke religious experience in a way that opens up the individual to the co-present gracious mystery of God. A sign of sound doctrine is its ability to communicate some aspect of the inexhaustible reality of God. A close interplay should obtain between theological doctrine and religious experience. This interplay will be both dialectical and analogical. Because of the nature of experience there will always be a certain tension between the richness of human experience and the historicity of doctrinal expression. The role of theology is to seek some kind of critical correspondence between doctrine and experience. A fundamental unity, therefore, should obtain in all instances between experience and doctrine. In this way the credibility of doctrine is advanced by reference to human experience and experience becomes the source of new religious knowledge. In particular this means that *the experience of God* entails some background *knowledge about God*.[58] This close relationship between religious experience and theological doctrine is clearly reflected in the theology of Rahner and Lonergan.

Rahner talks about the individual's transcendent experience of God through the experience of aloneness, freedom and responsibility, love and encounter, death and hope.[59] These experiences of transcendence are clarified for us through the categorical history of revelation which has culminated in Jesus as the Christ.[60] The later work of Rahner, in the 1960s and 1970s, has been an effort to keep these two realities of the experience of transcendence and divine revelation closely knit together.[61] In the end, Christianity for Rahner 'is none else but the deepest reality of transcendental experience, the experience of the absolute and forgiving nearness of God'.[62] Lonergan, in a similar vein, focuses upon the experience of the inner word of God flooding our hearts with love, which is expressed in the outer word of religious tradition.[63] This outer word which is made up of tradition, a fellowship that unites, and the Gospel that announces is constitutive in the coming to be of religious faith through experience.[64]

It should be noticed in passing that this emphasis on the intrinsic bond that exists between religious doctrine and religious experience reflects recent developments in epistemology. These developments insist that knowledge exists not in itself but always in relation to a conscious subject. The subject does not come to the knowledge by mere passive observation of how things are out there. Instead people like Michael Polanyi, a scientist, emphasise the personal participation of the knowing subject as essential to all acts of human understanding.[65] This element of personal participation is all the more important in the case of religious knowledge as bound up with human experience.

Criteria for Evaluating Religious Experience

Having examined what is involved in the appeal to experience in theology and having seen something about the complex character of religious experience and its unique relationship to doctrine, it is now necessary to outline some criteria for evaluating a religious understanding of common human experience. How are we to assess a religious interpretation of secular experience? On what grounds can we hold that there is a religious dimension implicit in human experience?

A number of theologians, Catholic (Schillebeeckx and Tracy) and Protestant (Ogden and Gilkey), respond to these questions by pointing out that an evaluation of the religious dimension of human experience should take place on two different levels.[66] On the other hand they suggest that it must be shown that a religious interpretation of experience is at least consistent with a secular understanding of life. This leads them to draw up what may be called 'criteria of adequacy.'[67] On the other hand these theologians also argue that it must be shown at the same time that this religious interpretation of experience is faithful to the demands of a specifically Christian understanding of existence.[68] This latter task gives rise to 'criteria of appropriateness'.[69] A remarkable degree of agreement exists among these theologians on the need for establishing and applying basic criteria in assessing the religious dimension of experience. In particular there is a strong apologetic concern to meet the demands of faith at all levels by showing that a religious understanding of experience does not contradict the creative aspirations of the secular spirit.

Concerning 'the criteria of adequacy' we will follow in broad outline the constructive framework proposed by David Tracy.[70] At the same time we will note the striking parallel that exists between Tracy's proposals and Schillebeeckx's treatment of the same issue.[71] Tracy suggests first of all that the religious interpretation of existence must be rooted in common human experience if it is to be meaningful. This criterion of meaningfulness requires that the religious dimension of life be related to 'the immediate lived experience of the self'[72] and that it disclose 'an authentic dimension of our experiences as selves'.[73] In the same spirit Schillebeeckx says that if religious language is to be meaningful, then we must ask: 'What aspect of ordinary human experience, which is shared by everybody or at least by very many people, is expressed in this use of language?'.[74] This relation of the religious understanding of life to lived experience replaces the old criteria of objective verification or falsification. Common human experience is the new empirical anchor for the meaningfulness of religious language.[75]

The next criterion of adequacy put forward by Tracy concerns the actual meaning of a religious understanding of experience. Here attention is focused on the cognitive claims being made. Can these claims be expressed conceptually in a way that is internally coherent?[76] Do these claims fit comfortably with the outlook of a secular community? At this level Schillebeeckx calls for an analysis of the language used to describe the religious dimension of experience. This analysis of religious language should take place at different levels: structural, logical, phenomenological and ontological.[77] The purpose of this elaborate linguistic analysis is substantially the same as that of Tracy: to ensure a conceptual coherence within the cognitive claims being made for the religious dimensions of experience in a way that does not clash with the established claims of a contemporary understanding of life. For example, the thesis developed above that God is co-present in human experience does not contradict the claims of the secular and scientific community.

The third criterion of adequacy recommended by Tracy concerns the issue of truth. The question must be asked whether the religious understanding of experience throws any light on the underlying conditions and presuppositions that make existence possible.[78] In particular this means finding out whether religious experience has anything to say to a secular person's fundamental trust and confidence in the worthwhileness of life. For Tracy the religious interpretation of experience represents, reassures and reaffirms humanity's basic trust and confidence in the value of existence, especially when it is called into question by negative experiences.[79] Again, a rather similar concern is found in Schillebeeckx who points out that people are united at a level of universal pre-understanding in their struggle to safeguard the *humanum* (the well being of humanity) and in their basic trust that good and not evil must have the last word. These two modes of universal pre-understanding should be endorsed by a religious interpretation of experience. Our common resistance against that which threatens the *humanum* is supported by a religious understanding of life which sees God as the ground of existence. In a similar way religious experience, specifically Christian religious experience, enables us to say that good not only 'must have' but 'will have' the last word.[80] In both instances a religious interpretation of experience confirms the pursuits of the secular community.

To summarise this first stage of a critical evaluation of religious experience, it can be said that the claims about the religious dimension of life should cohere with the shared experiences of others (meaningfulness), that they should be internally consistent at the conceptual level (meaning), and that they should confirm the underlying conditions for the possibility of existence within the secular and scientific world (true).

The application of these 'criteria of adequacy' should not be construed as a reduction of Christian theology to the norms of the secular world. What it does mean, however, is that the construction of theology for tomorrow, on the basis of these 'criteria of adequacy', will be spared the embarrassment of having to apologise for religious ideas that are at variance with the established findings of the modern, secular scientific community. Christian theology, to remain credible, must be safeguarded against idolatry, naive psychological projections, and the creation of a new 'God of the gaps'. In an address to the Pontifical Academy of Sciences Pope John Paul II points out that 'the critical spirit (of science) purifies it (religion) of a magical conception of the world and of surviving superstitions and exacts a more and more personal and active adherence to the faith.'[81] The 'criteria of adequacy' are designed to perform these tasks. Furthermore, the theologians who employ these 'criteria of adequacy' note explicitly that these criteria alone are insufficient; they must be complemented by Christian 'criteria of appropriateness'.[82]

Moving from the 'criteria of adequacy' to the 'criteria of appropriateness' it must be stated that the question of evaluation becomes more complex. Religious experience, though cognisant of the demands of the modern world, does not have an exact counterpart in the secular world. Religious experience, as should be clear by now, is unique and alone as a mode of experience. To bring out this special character of religious experience we will distinguish here between 'criteria of appropriateness' in the broad religious sense and 'criteria of appropriateness' in the specifically Christian sense. The purpose of this distinction is to focus on the shift and change that takes place at two levels in the move from 'criteria of adequacy' to 'criteria of appropriateness.'

The first criterion of appropriateness in the broad sense is: Does the encounter with the religious dimension of experience relate the individual to the power and presence of a Transcendent Reality worthy of total surrender in faith, absolute interest in hope and personal involvement in love? The emphasis here is bifocal. It is concerned on the one hand with the nature of the reality disclosed in religious experience and on the other hand with the personal participation of the subject in the final horizon of the experience. Is the experience such that it can become an object of ultimate concern (Tillich)? Is it sensed as a mystery that is both overpowering and fascinating (*mysterium tremendum et fascinans*) as Rudolp Otto expresses it?

Second, does the experience effect a genuine conversion in the life of the individual? This conversion must affect not only one's outlook but also one's behaviour patterns. The change must issue in some form of right action (*orthopraxis*) as well as adherence to beliefs.

Third, the religious experience must be found to chime in with the experiences of a particular religious community. Genuine religious experience cannot bypass the wisdom of community. This is especially important at a time when some are claiming 'special' religious experiences. Josiah Royce, the American philosopher, accurately points out in this regard that 'what's yours and only yours is not divine' (i.e. from God).

These three 'criteria of appropriateness' in the broad religious sense must now be further qualified in a specifically Christian way. This will entail taking account of the following points which can only be presented here in schematic outline:

1. The transcendent reality disclosed must be consonant with the incarnational revelation of God as Father in the person of his Son Jesus Christ through the power of the Holy Spirit. The experience must bring about a real *commitment* to the person of Jesus as the Christ who is the Word of God made flesh.

2. The religious experience should result in *decisions* inspired and informed by the vision of Jesus Christ. Such decisions would be influenced by the teaching of Jesus about realities like the kingdom of God, the Beatitudes and the new commandment of love.

3. The nature of the *conversion* should be both paschal and practical. It would be paschal by being patterned on the saving death and resurrection of Jesus which brought newness of life through death and light out of the darkness of the cross. It would have to be practical in terms of bringing about a transformation of the individual and society in the service of the Kingdom of God: 'By their fruits you will know them'.[83]

4. The religious experience needs to exist in some form of *continuity* with the experiences of the Christian community as expressed in Sacred Scripture and transmitted in the living tradition of that community. The task of determining this would rest with the recognised authority that resides within the Christian community.

5. The meaning of the religious experience should be compatible with the established Christian *regula fidei* (rules of faith). It would have to fit in, at least, with the hierarchy of truths and values that exists within Christianity. The existence of an overall coherence within the content of faith should also be taken into consideration.

6. The truth implicit in the religious experience should harmonise with the *eschatological understanding of reality* that is specific to Christianity. This would embrace the promise of a new heaven and a new earth centred in the kingdom of God to come.

In the light of these 'criteria of appropriateness', both religious and Christian, it should be clear that an evaluation of religious experience should take place within a circle of living religious faith. The nature of human contact with the religious dimension of secular experience is such that it cannot be detached or controlled in laboratory-like circumstances. Further, the elements of personal surrender and participation are essential to understanding the religious dimension of common, inclusive human experience.[84] Without a recognition of these perspectives the danger exists that God would seem to be present in human experience simply at the level of a postulated entity or inference. In addition, the dynamic, dialectical and transformative relationship that exists between faith and reason, understanding and believing, culture and commitment requires that the evaluation of religious experience take place within the circle of a religious community.

These criteria must not be taken as some kind of restriction imposed on the activity of God in the world. They are simply an index of what is required from the side of human beings in their response to God's permanent and active co-presence in the world.

THE EXPERIENCE OF GOD

The abundant grace of God cannot be confined to or captured by human criteria. And yet it is because the grace of God is so freely abundant that we must be scrupulously attentive in discerning God's omnipresence in human experience. *Noblesse oblige.*

In conclusion. it must be said that the continued centrality of experience in Protestant theology and its recovery in Catholic theology are important developments in the twentieth century. They are advances that will bring about a greater degree of personal participation by all in the exercise of theology. They should safeguard Christian theology from the temptation towards fundamentalism, intellectual objectivism, and doctrinal positivism. They should help to overcome any gap that may exist between life and theology as well as theory and practice. Lastly, they will provide critical foundations for the credibility of a theology of revelation and faith. Any developments which promote these goals in Christian theology must surely be welcomed and encouraged.

These criteria for the evaluation of religious experience may be summarised in the diagram overleaf.

QUESTIONS FOR DISCUSSION

1. Outline the meaning and ambiguity attached to the use of the word 'experience' in theology.

2. The experience of God is always a co-experience of a gracious presence already there, ahead of us, given in life, which is mediated to us by our interaction with creation, history, the lives of others and the Christian Community. Explain.

3. Show how our appreciation of what is going on in human experience depends on interpretation and imagination, and how interpretation in turn is closely bound up with language and the wisdom of the community.

CRITERIA FOR EVALUATING RELIGIOUS EXPERIENCE

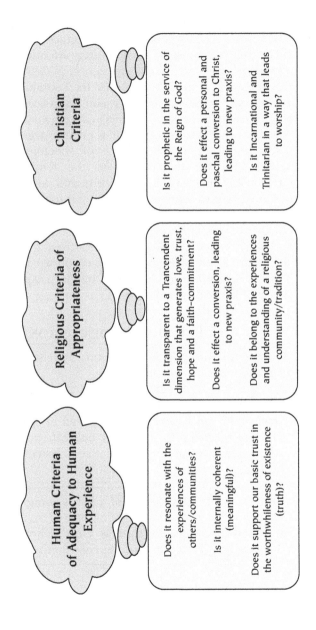

Christian Criteria

Is it prophetic in the service of the Reign of God?

Does it effect a personal and paschal conversion to Christ, leading to new praxis?

Is it Incarnational and Trinitarian in a way that leads to worship?

Religious Criteria of Appropriateness

Is it transparent to a Trancendent dimension that generates love, trust, hope and a faith-commitment?

Does it effect a conversion, leading to new praxis?

Does it belong to the experiences and understanding of a religious community/tradition?

Human Criteria of Adequacy to Human Experience

Does it resonate with the experiences of others/communities?

Is it internally coherent (meaningful)?

Does it support our basic trust in the worthwhileness of existence (truth)?

Recommended Readings

Articles:

- Carr, Anne, 'Theological Anthropology and the Experience of Women', Anne E. Carr, *Transforming Grace: Christian Tradition and Women's Experience*, San Francisco: Harper and Row, 1988.
- Tracy, David, 'The Return of God in Contemporary Theology', *Concilium* 1994/6, edited by W. Jeanrond and C. Geffré.
- MacKinnon, Mary Heather, 'Experience and God', *Readings in Ecology and Feminist Theology*, Edited by Mary H. MacKinnon and Moni McIntyre, Kansas City: Sheed and Ward, 1995
- Lane, Dermot A., 'Theology in Transition', *Catholic Theology Facing the Future: Historical Perspectives,* Edited by Dermot A. Lane, Dublin/New York: Columba Books/Paulist Press, 2003.

Books:

- Thomas M. Kelly, *Theology at the Void: The Retrieval of Experience,* Indiana: University of Notre Dame Press, 2002.
- Charles Taylor, *Varieties of Religion Today*, Massachusetts: Harvard University Press, 2002.
- Gallagher, Michael P., *Clashing Symbols: An Introduction to Faith and Culture,* revised edition, London: DLT, 2003.

2

THE NATURE OF REVELATION

Revelation and faith are correlative. In this human response (faith), the primary linguistic carriers of the revelatory event are generally more akin to poetry than to precise prose, since it is in the poetic mode that language finds its highest possibilities ... Indeed, narrative holds pride of place in the expression of revelation precisely because this genre is most appropriate to human beings as essentially temporal human beings ... Divine revelation is not information but a gift that entails a command to do the truth. (Michael J. Scanlon)[1]

May I set ajar
The doors of closed minds. Words come and words go
And poetry is pain as well as passion
But in the large flights of imagination
I see for one crammed second order so
Explicit that I need no more persuasion (Elizabeth Jennings)[2]

Good theology is indispensable to the life of the Church. It is informed by a searching fidelity to God's revelation in Jesus Christ expressed in the Bible and the living tradition of the Church. Theology in the normal course of events assumes the existence and giveness of revelation. For that reason theology is as strong or as weak as its understanding of revelation is. It is important, however, from time to time to review the underlying pre-suppositions of a science even though such an exercise tends to make some people feel uneasy. There is nothing more vulnerable in life than unquestioned presuppositions. Theology is keenly aware of the need to be self-critical of its own grounds Indeed a special branch of theology, fundamental theology, deals specifically with its own presuppositions and foundations. A key area in fundamental theology is the question of revelation.

The state of theology at any one time in the life of the Church depends in large measure on the healthy condition of its presuppositions. If these presuppositions are firmly grounded, then theology will advance imaginatively through a process of critical fidelity to the creative Word of God. On the other hand, if there is disagreement about these presuppositions then there will be tension in the exercise of theology. Some of the tensions today in the life of the Church are caused by misunderstandings about the nature of revelation.

The nature of revelation was discussed and debated at length during the Second Vatican Council. A change and development in the Church's theological understanding took place at that Council.[3] Anyone who doubts this statement should compare the first schema drawn up on revelation at the Council in 1962 with the finally approved text promulgated in 1965. Commentators on the Council's *Dogmatic Constitution on Divine Revelation (Dei verbum)* are agreed that a significant shift of emphasis in the understanding of revelation occurred at Vatican II.[4]

Whenever a change in focus occurs, especially in an area of fundamental theology, it takes time for the Christian community to adjust to its implications. The period of adjustment can be one of pain and tension, especially between those who, on the one hand, have come to grips with the shift in perspective and those, on the other hand, who find it difficult to move forward from previously held strong positions. Such pain and tension are in evidence at present in the life of the Church. One of the causes, not always recognised as such, is the new thinking in the Church concerning the nature of revelation.

For some, revelation appears primarily as a clear deposit of truths to be jealously guarded and defensively protected by the

Church. This particular view of revelation was taken up at the Second Vatican Council and supplemented by another and more important view on revelation. One way of capturing this advance in the Church's self-understanding of revelation and its significance for theology today is to review the current state of thinking on revelation. The purpose of this chapter is to do just that. We will confine ourselves to the nature and process of revelation. This will entail a critical analysis of recent views on revelation, followed by an outline of some basic theological principles, a description of different types of revelation and a summary of the unique contribution of Vatican II to the theology of revelation.

Different Theories of Revelation

The question of revelation concerns the way God has disclosed God's self to humanity in history, especially in the history of the people of Israel and the person of Jesus. Assuming the experience of God as outlined in Chapter One, the theology of revelation sets out to narrate the story of God's activity in the world and to describe how people have experienced and responded in faith to this divine presence. Different theories have arisen to explain this saving encounter and historical interaction between God and human beings.

Certainly the most popular theory is that which has come to be called 'the propositional view'. It claims that God communicated basic truths, hitherto unknown, about God's self in history to a privileged people, and that these were written down in a human language and passed on in Scripture and the tradition of the Church. A kind of divine verbal communication took place between God and the world in the history of the people of Israel and the life of Jesus. The agents of this divine communication were the prophets and the apostles who were regarded as the messengers of God. Revelation in this view is seen as God speaking to the individual (*locutio Dei*). Scripture is understood to contain the literal Word of God. Most theologians today are uneasy with an exclusively propositional view of revelation.[5] It is pointed out, especially in the light of historical studies into the Bible, that the prophets and the apostles did not arrive at their insights about God simply as a result of divine dictation. The account of revelation in the books of the Bible clearly reflects the historical, social and cultural circumstances of the time of their composition. Further, the faith of the prophets and the apostles obviously played an active part in shaping the content of revelation contained in Scripture. The dividing line between the Word of God and the word of human beings is by no means as clear as this theory suggests. More serious, however, is the suggestion that the revelation of God could be reduced to a series of propositions to which the individual must give assent in faith. The living reality of God in history is more than a body of frozen truths. God cannot be confined to or captured by a simple set of propositions. Lastly, the verbal view of revelation seems to imply that the communication of God to people has stopped and that God has thus withdrawn from the world, leaving the human race bereft of any further divine traces. Such a view of revelation seems to contradict the important doctrine of God's co-presence to the world outlined in Chapter One and the indwelling of the Spirit within the Christian community.

Because of these difficulties with the propositional view of revelation a second theory was put forward, called the 'revelation as history' theory.[6] This focuses on the facts of history. Revelation is about the action of God in history which is available to us in the great events of salvation history. The revelation of God takes place through the mighty acts of God in the history of the chosen people and the person of Jesus. Revelation is a series of different historical events which are 'open to anyone who has eyes to see'.[7]

This view of revelation, it could be argued, as put forward by the Pannenberg circle and others, is an improvement on the propositional account of revelation. Yet it also has difficulties. For one thing it seems to suggest that the great events of history are self-evident in regard to their revelatory import. In fact, however, a neutral or detached historian would not find the events of Israel's history more revelatory of God than the events of any other nation's history.[8] In addition, the role of faith in the process of discerning revelation is played down too much. The perception of revelation in history seems to be a matter simply of scientific investigation and rational discovery. Further, the elements of divine grace and offer are not sufficiently taken into account among the 'revelation as history' school.

By way of reaction against these two views yet another theory of revelation has been put forward. This third theory may be loosely designated as the subjectivist or existentialist theory of revelation. It points out that too much attention is given in the above theories to the objective reality of God's self-revelation and that not enough emphasis is placed on the faith dispositions of the individual who receives revelation. It is claimed that revelation takes place only when humanity responds in faith to God's message contained in the Bible. This happens when Scripture actually changes and transforms the life of the person. The Word of God in Scripture calls us to a faith-decision; it opens our eyes in the present moment to the co-presence of God in the world and history. Revelation is not about digging up doctrinal information about God from the past. Instead it is about a personal existential faith-decision here and now.[9]

Like the other two views this theory has some value but it also contains real limitations. It reduces revelation simply to the level of a faith-decision. It concentrates too much on the present aspect of revelation to the neglect of revelation in the past. In doing so it creates something of a divorce between present faith and past history. Further, it diminishes the givenness of revelation simply to the level of a personal faith-decision. It neglects the role of tradition as the bearer and the Christian community as the interpreter of God's self revelation to humanity.

The principal difficulty with each of these three theories is one of incompleteness. Each theory does contain an important aspect about God's revelation. A balanced theology of revelation must attempt to integrate these three complementary points of view as well as add to them. Of course revelation is about words, and deeds, and faith, and many other elements. The point at issue in any theology of revelation is: How exactly is the revelation of God made known in faith to the individual? Where precisely is the point of contact between God's address and the person's response in faith? Does the communication between God and the individual belong exclusively to the past, or does it also include the present in some way or other? How does one safeguard the graciousness of

THE EXPERIENCE OF GOD

God's action in history and at the same time respect the free response in faith of the individual? To answer these questions we must first of all draw up some basic theological principles.

Principles for a Theology of Revelation

If we are to appreciate the process of revelation between God and the individual it is important from the start that we understand what is involved in the dynamics of human revelation between people. It is reasonable to assume that God in divine revelation follows, more or less, the built-in created capacity that humanity has for human revelation. God deals with people as they are. He takes the human condition as it is and draws it to perfection in grace. The gift of grace does not bypass nature; it develops from within nature. From the human points of view we can say that revelation is a personal, relational and 'dialogical' category. It involves an interpersonal exchange in which each of the participants grows into a condition of mutual trust, confidence and communication. Human revelation entails a process of self-disclosure between persons that normally takes place through words and deeds. This communication between people reaches a special level of integrity when the words become deeds and the deeds reflect the words in unity. If the exchange is to be complete, then there must be some mutual interaction between the parties involved. This takes place through the medium of human experience which is essential to revelation. An initiative is taken from one side, an offer is made, an invitation is issued which in turn requires a response, an acceptance and acknowledgement if there is to be genuine communication and revelation. When this interpersonal exchange occurs there results a new awareness which comes as gift, answering a real need and bringing about a change in the recipient. This new level of consciousness expresses itself in the language of love and relationship. These basic elements which make up the dynamics of human revelation also belong, with some qualification, to the process of divine revelation between God and humanity.

The next important principle belonging to a theology of revelation is that a fundamental unity exists between revelation and faith. There can be no divine revelation without the response of faith which receives it, and there can be no faith without the grace of God's self revelation which draws forth faith in us. The revelation of God only becomes effective through the active engagement in faith of the individual. This demands that we move away from a spectator view of revelation as if it were just a matter of providing a replay of the past. Instead revelation is not available in terms of a television action-replay; instead revelation is only available in terms of a faith understanding of the biblical and ecclesial witness. The element of personal participation is integral to the experience of revelation. Personal participation implies that there is both an objective and a subjective dimension to every experience of revelation. Indeed, there must be a developed degree of human subjectivity if genuine objectivity is to be reached in the process of revelation.[10]

Without a response in faith, revelation remains at the level of an unrecognised gift and an unacknowledged invitation. In other words, there is no real revelation for the individual until it has been received in faith. The reception in faith of God's gracious offer of God's self in experience and history by the individual, and ultimately by the community, is what constitutes revelation. A proportionate relationship, therefore, exists between the response of the individual in faith and the content of revelation.

In recent times some theologians have argued for the primacy of faith over revelation.[11] It is suggested that revelation is an extension of the language of faith. To talk in this way gives the impression of setting up a false opposition and rivalry between revelation and faith. Further, it seems to imply that faith could exist without revelation or at least in separation from revelation. The revelation of God to the person in human experience and language is more than simply a creation by faith that interprets life 'as if' one had contact with God. To be sure revelation is only available in the language of faith but this does not mean that revelation is simply an outgrowth of faith. Faith and the language of faith originate out of the experience of God's active power and presence in history, that is, out of revelation. Revelation, therefore, is the source of religious faith. One cannot separate the revelation of God to the person in experience from the faith which receives it, nor can one isolate faith from the revelation that generates it in experience.[12] The Word of God is by no means reducible to human language. The primacy of God's grace within the unity that exists between divine revelation and faith must be maintained.

Arising out of this relationship that exists between revelation and faith is the question of human experience. The locus of God's revelation is human experience. The primary point of contact between God and the individual in history is human experience. The medium of revelation, therefore, is human experience.[13] The revelation of God in history takes place in human experience. The search for God outside human experience has rightly been described as a search for idols.[14] This particular emphasis on experience is a reaction against abstract and overly intellectualistic approaches in the past to revelation. It also highlights the need for some degree of active awareness and self-consciousness in the recipient who appropriates God's revelation.[15] It is only with the emergence of self-consciousness which takes place in the crucible of human experience that we are ready to receive and capable of discerning divine revelation. The revelation of God in history is always addressed to human self-consciousness and as such draws self-consciousness out of its lonely isolation into a new liberating relationship and communion with God. Consciousness of ourselves before and in the presence of God is quite different from consciousness of ourselves without reference to God. The revelation of God does in fact change our consciousness. It is only in and through the revelation of God that we become fully conscious of ourselves, of our origin and our destiny. The field of this divine activity is experience, or, better, religious experience. To this extent faith is always a response based on, derived from, and inspired by the experience of the revelation of God. The essential link between the revelation of God and the faith of humanity is human experience.

Following the principles of Chapter One we must distinguish here, however briefly, between ordinary everyday experience, a depth experience and religious experience (see diagram on p.25). As already noted, ordinary experiences are concerned with the visible empirical world of objects 'out there'. Depth experiences bring us into the invisible but real world mediated by meaning: truth, beauty, and love. Religious experiences are those moments in life when we perceive a world of meaning as grounded in that immanent and yet transcendent reality we call God. In experiencing the world mediated by meaning, we can co-experience the presence of God as the source of that meaning. Religious experience is a particular configuration and interpretation of depth experiences. A religious experience, therefore, is always an experience of something else at one and the same time.[16] It is a phenomenon of co-knowing and co-experiencing God in human knowledge and experience of personal existence in the world. Thus it must be asserted clearly that there is no such thing as a chemically pure religious experience that brings about an unambiguous revelation. Depth experiences of truth, of beauty, and of meaning have the capacity to be at the same time religious experiences. A religious experience, for our purpose here, may be described as a revelatory experience of God. Every revelatory experience, therefore, is always alloyed with human and historical elements which provide the ambience of contact between God and humanity. Thus revelation is always mediated. There is no unmediated revelation of God in the sense of words spoken directly by God, nor are there direct theophanies which manifest God *in se*. In more traditional language one might say that revelation is symbolic, incarnational, and sacramental. As symbolic, incarnational, and sacramental, revelation is, therefore, experiential.

This emphasis on experience as the locus of revelation does not mean that we can now identify the revelation of God to us simply with human experience. Rather we are suggesting that revelation always takes place in and through the medium of human experience. This does not imply that revelation is reducible to human experience. Revelation begins in human experience and takes us beyond experience to that deeper divine dimension we call the mystery of God at the centre of life. A revelatory experience is a human experience seen through the power of imagination in its full breadth and depth. The God who reveals God's self through human experience is both immanent and transcendent. The transcendence of God is discovered through the immanence of God which addresses us in human experience. This transcendence of God constantly reminds us that there is more to be known about the mystery than we have experienced in life. Every revelation of God contains at the same time an element of concealment about God.

The revelation of God in experience is something that cries out for imaginative interpretation in linguistic symbols: narratives, stories and doctrinal statements. In fact interpretation assisted by imagination is an essential part of the revelation of God in experience. A fundamental unity exists between experience, imagination, and interpretation. Where experience ends and the complimentary roles of imagination and interpretation begin is extremely difficult, if not impossible, to delineate. The imaginative words of interpretation spring up out of the community which discerns the revelatory significance of human experience. The revelation of God to the individual is shaped by the religious community and its traditions. For the Christian, the final word of interpretation of experience is provided by Jesus as the Word of God Incarnate. In turn, scripture, tradition and the authority of the Christian community provide the guiding words of interpretation of God's Revelation.

This access to God in revelation through human experience takes place in history. The unique contribution of Wolfhart Pannenberg to the theology of revelation has undoubtedly been his emphasis on history which he describes as the comprehensive horizon of Christian theology. The full revelation of God will only be complete at the end of history. That end of history has been anticipated, for Pannenberg, in the resurrection of Jesus from the dead.[17]

World-history is the primary context for understanding salvation-history. It was the isolation of salvation-history into some kind of super-history that was largely responsible for the distortion of special revelation into a block of divine truths. Salvation-history as the vehicle of Judaeo-Christian Revelation is a particular faith-perception of what is going on in universal history.[18] The response, interpretation and imaginative expression of faith in relation to the co-presence of God in history is the story of revelation.

Two distinct attitudes concerning the interplay between revelation and history are discernible. Some argue that the faith response of the person is the crucial moment in revelation-history. It is faith that creates salvation-history out of universal history. In effect the special revelation of Judaism could just as well have taken place in Greece as in Israel. There is nothing very special, therefore, about the historical events of Israel besides the particular Jewish faith interpretation of them. Others suggest that God intervenes directly in history in a way that compels faith. In this case salvation-history appears as a series of unmistakable divine interventions and miraculous events in history.[19] The former position neglects the givenness of salvation-history and the latter ignores the freedom of faith. In both instances the unity that obtains between revelation and history is severed. The givenness of God's revelation in salvation-history is available in the faith of the people of Israel and Christian community.[20] Revelation is always mediated and incarnated in history,[21] but this must not blind us to the truth that a real experience and exchange did take place between God and humanity in the history of Israel and Jesus. On the other hand, salvation-history is the special history of a particular people's faith. It is not the history of naked divine acts or historical events. All history is history interpreted imaginatively. Salvation-history is history experienced and interpreted imaginatively within a particular faith perspective. This fundamental principle, already reflected in the unity that exists between revelation and faith, must be taken seriously in regard to all aspects of revelation, including its historical dimensions. It is only by constantly returning to this basic principle that we will avoid a crude approach to God's self-revelation in experience and avoid a literal understanding of the Word of God.

Universal, Jewish and Christian Revelation

It is against the background of these basic principles that we can now begin to look more directly at the process of revelation in experience and language. Most people associate the word 'revelation' with the special revelation of God in the history of Judaism and Jesus Christ. However, there is another equally important aspect of God's revelation which is too often neglected. This is 'natural' revelation, or what some call universal or general revelation, or others refer to as cosmic revelation. Neglect of this aspect of revelation is the cause of many problems that people have with special revelation. Indeed it is very difficult to work out a theology of Judaeo-Christian revelation that does not take account of universal revelation. In fact universal and cosmic revelation is the backdrop against which special and particular revelation makes sense. Without this backdrop special revelation is in danger of being isolated and appearing extrinsic and, therefore, unrelated to mainstream of life itself.

Universal revelation is about the primary communication of God to human beings that takes place in the experience of faith through contact with creation, human existence and other people. Such revelation is universal in the sense that it does not depend on a particular place in the world or time in history.

The experience of creation embraces our contact with the world around us as a single organic reality. It includes our relationship with the rhythm of nature pulsating with life, the different cycles of life and the seasons of the year. The kind of experience we have in mind here is summed up by Gerald Manley Hopkins in the statement: 'The world is charged with the grandeur of God' or in the words of Elizabeth B. Browning:

> Earth is crammed with heaven,
> and every common bush afire with God;
> But only we who sees
> Takes off his shoes
> While all the rest gather blackberries
> ('Auror Leigh')

Increasingly the cosmic dimensions of God's revelation are coming to the fore in the light of new cosmologies and astrophysics. One can hardly remain unmoved by the emerging vastness of the cosmos and the smallness of the earth that humans inhabit.

The experience of existence is always something personal to every human being and yet there are fundamental elements in this experience of existence that all people undergo which can be revelatory. These would include the experience of the contingency of human existence,[22] the dynamic drive toward transcendence[23], the innate moral impulse, and the immensity of the universe we find ourselves in, all of which are fundamental characteristics of the human condition. Such experiences of contingency, transcendence, conscience, and cosmic consciousness bring us into contact with joy and sorrow, life and death, fulfilment and frustration, good and evil. The orientation of these experiences is hinted at by Augustine when he claims that 'the heart is restless till it finds its rest in thee (God)' and by Aquinas who talks about the 'instinct of faith'[24] which is graciously endowed upon every human spirit.

The experience of encounter with 'the other', especially the face of the other, is unique among human experiences and often results in a strong sense of summons and call. In particular, the experience of the face of the other makes irresistible moral demands as well as opening up a disclosure of depth that flows from a selfless 'I-thou' exchange. Something of this experience is caught in the assertion by Irenaeus that 'the human person fully alive is the glory of God'. These different experiences throw up a pattern in life that cannot be ignored or dodged: fragments of meaning, splinters of beauty, and hazy glimpses of truth are disclosed. Such experiences invite us to acknowledge an underlying ground to these fragments of meaning, a source for beauty, and an acceptance of an origin for these glimpses of truth. This ground, source, and origin invite a response of faith. This universal revelation gives rise to basic religious faith in that graciously immanent and yet transcendent reality we call God. Such universal revelation gives rise to basic religious faith. The precise content of that basic faith is often vague and ill-defined. It amounts, at least, to an acceptance of reality as ultimately meaningful, an acknowledgement of the universe as 'friendly', and an affirmation that life is rooted in some kind of unknown but real superior being or power or spirit or force or mystery which we identify with God. The response in faith to the demands and implications of these fundamental core-experiences is the beginning of universal revelation.

Applying the principles already enunciated above, it could be argued that the experience of cosmos is God's primary word or language to us and that the gift of personal existence is God's initial deed in regard to us. This primary word and initial deed of God come together into a single invitation from God which is mediated to us through our experience of creation and 'the other' who is the image of God in the world. Evidence for the existence of universal revelation is clearly available in biblical and Church traditions. For example in the Old Testament Scriptures the psalmist reminds us that 'the heavens proclaim the glory of God'. The classic example in the New Testament is St Paul who tells us in Romans 1:20:

> Ever since the creation of the world his invisible nature, namely his eternal power and deity, has been perceived in the things that have been made.

Preaching to the unbelievers at Lystra Paul is able to point out that God

> did not leave himself without witness, for he did good and gave you from heaven rains and fruitful seasons; satisfying your hearts with truth and gladness (Acts 14:17).

In a similar vein the Second Vatican Council acknowledges

- that 'other religions reflect a ray of divine truth'

- that from 'ancient times there have existed among diverse peoples a perception of that hidden power which hovers over the course of things and over the events of human life'.[25]

- that people should seek 'to uncover with gladness and respect those seeds of the word which lie hidden among' ... 'national and religious traditions'[26]

Ultimately, the existence of universal revelation is implied by the Christian doctrine of the universal saving will of God. The saving grace of God in the world is universal and, therefore, to that extent it follows that the revelation of God is universal. If grace is universal then revelation is also universal.[27]

From the existence of universal, cosmic revelation we can now move on to the special, historical revelation of Judaism and

Christianity. The basic religious faith evoked by universal revelation is the context or background of entry into Jewish revelation. The development of this basic faith into a particular form and content arose out of the Jewish experience of God in history. The precise origin, form and content of that faith is too complex to elaborate in detail here.

At a minimum it includes the presence of a strong monotheism, a particular view of history, a covenant-creational relationship with God in history, and the emergence of hope-filled promises about the future of history. In contrast to its polytheistic neighbours, Judaic faith affirmed a lively monotheism. The association of this monotheism with the movements of history gave rise to the emergence of the Jewish people as a distinct religious group. For Israel, their God, Yahweh, was active in a particular way through history. History was understood as something linear, having a beginning, a middle and an end joined by the continuous activity of God, whereas for other religious groups history was largely cosmological, simply repeating itself in a circle without any goal. In contrast Jewish history gradually unfolded as something meaningful and filled with promises for the Jews with a definite purpose according to a particular plan. The guiding principle of history was God. The Jewish people came to know God through their experience of history. The revelation of God to the Jewish people, therefore, took place primarily in the drama of history.

For the Jews God was active in their history, initiating their history in the past through the call of Abraham their father in faith, bringing them together into a new relationship described in terms of covenant, and leading them forth in hope with promises for the future. The basic historical events in Judaism were the call of Abraham, the exodus from Egypt, the covenant at Sinai, the Babylonian captivity and the return from exile. Taken together, these historical events disclosed a pattern of God being present and absent to them as Lord of their history. They revealed God to the chosen people as a loving, faithful, sometimes angry, always forgiving, and ever-present God. Their God was a God, historically active, personally concerned and passionately involved with God's people (Ex 3:7-10). The interpretation of these historical experiences was undertaken imaginatively by the prophets and summarised into basic statements of faith: 'The Lord God has brought us out of Egypt with a mighty hand.' Gradually Jewish creeds, such as 'a wandering Aramean was my father...' (Dt 26:5ff; cf. also Dt 16:20ff: Jos 24:ff) and ethical codes of behaviour summed up in the commandments like 'Worship no God but me...' (Dt 5:7ff) emerged. Eventually these oral traditions were committed to writing under the direction of the elders of the Jewish community giving us the Hebrew Scriptures.

These different historical events should not be seen simply as direct interventions from the outside which forced faith as it were. Instead they were real but natural historical events which carried and contained extraordinary divine significance for the chosen people in virtue of their personal and communal faith participation in these events. It was the unique and particular religious consciousness of Israel that enabled them to discern the hand of God acting in their history.[28] It was the content of what was revealed in faith and not so much the way of revealing that was extraordinary.[29] This means that we must be careful not to confuse or identify the extraordinary Jewish faith perception of history simply with the original events of history. To the outsider these historical events would appear simply at the level of natural events. One cannot say 'There, that's an act of God in history' or 'This is revelation' in isolation from the faith that enables one to make such statements. This does not mean, however, that the revelation of God in Judaism is simply the creation of faith. God was personally active and present in the history of the chosen people in a way that generated a specific Jewish faith response. As already noted above, the greater the faith response to the presence of God revealing God's self, the deeper the revelation of God to the individual and the community.

This unique interaction between God and humans in the history of Judaism is summed up in the central doctrine of the covenant: 'I will be your God and you will be my people' (Jer 31:33; Ezek 36:28). The covenant is about the special relationship that exists between God and Israel. It expresses the Jewish faith understanding of God's self-revelation to the people of Israel as chosen. This covenant relationship between God and God's people, based on historical experiences, is in time extended backwards to embrace the whole of creation. Within Judaism the act of creation by God is part of salvation and revelation history.[30] Creation is included in God's special covenant relationship with God's people. The God of the historical Sinaitic covenant is also the Creator-God of the whole world.[31] It was this understanding of creation as an essential element of God's covenant and saving history that distinguished Judaism and its understanding of God in history from the other religions of the Near East with their creation-myth stories.[32] Indeed the key to Jewish revelation is the covenant, and essential elements of that covenant between God and the individual are creation, history and the Law (*Torah*).

As a result of these different historical experiences of God there grew up within Judaism certain expectations which were based on memories of the past. In time these forward-looking expectations hardened into promises which issued in new hopes. These promises centred upon the establishment of a new and eternal covenant (Jer 32:36ff.) as well as the restoration of 'a new heart and a new mind' (Ex 36:26) to Israel and the creation of a kingdom of justice and peace (Is 9:2-7; 11:1-9). The central figure associated with the realisation of these expectations was the Messiah who would be the anointed one of Yahweh. Different messianic expectations emerged. Some saw the Messiah as a royal kingly figure following in the footsteps of David (Is 9:1-7; 11:1-9; Zech 3:6-10; 4:6-14). Others saw the Messiah as a priestly person who would bring about the restoration of worship in the temple (Hag 2:1-9; Mal 3:1-4; Ez 40-44; 1 Chr 22-26). In addition, there were those who expected the Messiah to be a prophetic figure (Dt 18:15-18; 1 Mac 4:41-50; 14:41; Mal 3:1ff; Sir 48:10). Lastly, some looked to the coming of a suffering servant of Yahweh who would heal the ills of Israel through suffering (Is 42:1-4; 45:1-7; 50:4-11; 52:3-53:12).

This bare outline of Judaic revelation is the backdrop against which Christian revelation takes place. Within this context, the experience of the public ministry, death and resurrection of Jesus by the apostles constitutes the climax and summation of God's involvement in history. Jesus Christ is the personal revelation of God to people. The Christ-event is the fullness of God's self-communication to humanity in history. The life of Jesus is the anticipation and transformation of Jewish hopes.

Jesus is the anticipation of Jewish expectations in the sense that the promised future of Israel has been realised in the personal life, death and resurrection of Jesus (Acts 13:33-39). A new and eternal covenant in the blood of Christ has been established. The kingdom of God (a kingdom of justice and peace and love) has been inaugurated through the saving death and resurrection of Jesus. A new creation has been instituted: 'If anyone is in Christ, he is a new creation; the old has passed away; behold the new has come' (2 Cor 5:17). Thus St Paul can write:

> For all the promises of God find their yes in him. That's why we utter 'Amen' through him to the glory of God (2 Cor 1:20).

Jesus is also the transformation of Jewish hopes in virtue of the fact that these now exist on a new and different level. Because the risen Christ is 'the first fruits of those who have fallen asleep' (1 Cor 15:20), the grounds of hope have been explicitated and enlarged. A down payment, as it were, has been made ensuring the future hope of humanity so that now we believe that 'in Christ all shall be made alive' (1 Cor 15:22). In the light of Jesus as the Christ who has conquered death through resurrection, the seeds of a new hope have been sown that will blossom forth when he returns in glory to complete what he has set in motion (1 Cor 15:23-24).

In addition, Christ and all that he stands for is now the centre of history and creation. The course and direction of history have been altered by the life, death and resurrection of Jesus. We have been given a preview of the end through the resurrection of Jesus crucified. The *Pastoral Constitution on the Church in the Modern World* sums up the revelatory significance of Jesus in the following way:

> The Lord (Jesus Christ) is the goal of human history, the focal point of the longings of history and civilisation, the centre of the human race, the joy of every heart and the answer to all its yearnings.[33]

Further, the person of Jesus Christ as the Word Incarnate is the revelation of God to humanity and of humanity to the world.

Christ reveals the reality of God as Father and his love; he makes 'all ... see what is the plan of the mystery hidden for all ages in God' (Eph 3:9). At the same time 'he fully reveals the human to humanity and makes his or her supreme calling clear'.[34] The destiny of the individual is disclosed in the risen Christ who is now the future of the individual. 'In Christ you will discover the greatness of your humanity.'[35] As the revelation of God and the human, Jesus is also the perfect response to God's offer of love as well as the personal embodiment and bearer of God's invitation to women and men alike.

Not only is Christian revelation the crystalisation of Judaic revelation, but it also illuminates our understanding of universal revelation. Christ is 'the light of the world' (Jn 8:12) and the 'Word made flesh' (Jn 1:14). As such the revelation of God in Jesus lights up what is going on in the world around us. The particularity of the Christ-event is the personalisation and concentration of the universal revelation of God in creation, human existence and other people. The universal interaction between God and humanity has been specified and exemplified in Jesus of Nazareth. To that extent Christian revelation is normative for a proper understanding of the ongoing universal revelation of God in the world.

What is unique and distinctive about the revelation of God in Jesus is the claim that this revelation is first and foremost the personal revelation of God. The reality of Jesus reveals the personal presence and activity of God in history. What happened in Jesus is much more than a gnostic-like communication of special truths about God; the person of Jesus is *una persona* with God;[36] Jesus is true God and truly human at one and the same time. In other religions revelation may consist in the propositional communication of secrets and special information about God whereas in Christianity we are dealing with the personal gift of God's self in the reality of Jesus.[37] For the Christian the primary emphasis is placed on the personal revelation of God that takes place in Jesus. Jesus is the personal revelation of God not in virtue of this or that particular deed, but in virtue of the truth that Jesus is personally the Son of God made flesh in history. It is this which enabled the early Church to say that to see Jesus Christ is to see God and to hear the word of Jesus Christ is to hear the Word of God.

THE EXPERIENCE OF GOD

In addition, the uniqueness and distinctiveness of Christian revelation must include particular reference to the death and resurrection of Jesus. The cross and exaltation of Jesus is a powerful symbolic statement to the effect that, in spite of indications to the contrary, suffering, evil and death do not have the last word. Further, the crucified and risen Christ is the eschatological event in history; it is the realisation of God's promises and humanity's hopes in history. The individual resurrection of Jesus from the dead anticipates the end of time (the *eschaton*) and in doing so points humanity in a new and radical way toward the future. The horizons of hope have been expanded by the resurrection of Jesus to embrace the future possibility of 'a new heaven and a new earth' (Rev 21:1) as an essential element of the new creation already established in Christ Jesus (2 Cor 5:17; Gal 6:15).[38] The different kinds of revelation may be summarised as follows:

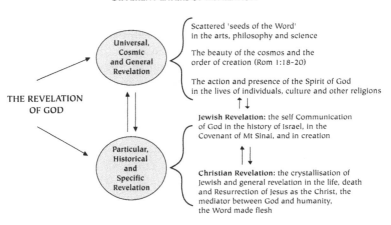

DIFFERENT LAYERS OF REVELATION

THE REVELATION OF GOD

Universal, Cosmic and General Revelation

Scattered 'seeds of the Word' in the arts, philosophy and science

The beauty of the cosmos and the order of creation (Rom 1:18-20)

The action and presence of the Spirit of God in the lives of individuals, culture and other religions

Particular, Historical and Specific Revelation

Jewish Revelation: the self Communication of God in the history of Israel, in the Covenant of Mt Sinai, and in creation

Christian Revelation: the crystallisation of Jewish and general revelation in the life, death and Resurrection of Jesus as the Christ, the mediator between God and humanity, the Word made flesh

The Insights of Vatican II on Revelation

Our reflections so far on revelation could be said to represent the mainstream of developments in Catholic theology during the late twentieth century. Much of this thinking is summed up and reflected in the *Dogmatic Constitution on Divine Revelation (Dei verbum)*, which came out of the Second Vatican Council in 1965. In this final section we will draw together the principal insights of *Dei verbum* by way of illustration and confirmation of the above theology of revelation. We will confine ourselves to Chapter I, which is concerned with the nature of revelation and which is the principal focus of this chapter.

To appreciate the change in perspective that took place in the Church's self-understanding of revelation at the Second Vatican Council we must begin with a brief outline of the teaching of the First Vatican Council on revelation in 1870. Vatican I was the first Council to deal formally and explicitly with the theme of revelation. Prior to that, individual points about revelation had been dealt with in passing. The decree from Vatican I, *Dei Filius*, deals with the mystery of God, revelation, faith and reason. The immediate background to this decree was the existence of fideism and rationalism stemming from the Enlightenment as well as certain forms of deism. Against fideism it asserted the power of human reason to know God through reflection on created realities. In opposition to rationalism it affirmed the existence of supernatural revelation and the absolute necessity of this revelation for a proper understanding of the final end of the person. Within this context it talked about supernatural revelation in terms of the communication of divine mysteries, the doctrine of the faith, the deposit of faith and revealed truths.[39] A sharp distinction was made between natural and supernatural revelation.[40] Very little reference was made to the person of Christ as the source of revelation. The major emphasis was on revelation as a body of truths that have been handed down in Scripture and tradition. Yet it would be inaccurate to claim that Vatican I opted exclusively for a propositional view of revelation. It does state, in a rarely noticed sentence, that it pleased God 'to reveal himself and the eternal decrees of his will'.[41] Yet in spite of this it must be admitted that the predominant horizon of Vatican I on revelation was that which identified revelation with a body of supernatural truths.

It is against this background that we must read the *Dogmatic Constitution on Divine Revelation* from the Second Vatican Council. Without this point of comparison much of the richness and significance of *Dei verbum* would be lost. What is perhaps most instructive about the Second Vatican Council on revelation is that the first draft of the decree in 1962 incorporated the primary emphasis of Vatican I on revelation as a body of truth, whereas the final text of 1965, which came after four further drafts, presented revelation in a new and different perspective.[42] This does not mean that Vatican II overthrew the teaching of Vatican. To the contrary a conscious effort is made in Vatican II to maintain links with Vatican I. This is quite explicit in the opening article of *Dei verbum* which declares that Vatican II is following in the footsteps of Vatican I. It is also clear, for example, in the last section of Chapter I which is made up of a mosaic of quotations from Vatican I.

In broad terms we can say that the Second Vatican Council, in *Dei verbum*, sees revelation as the personal self-communication of God to people in the history of salvation which reaches its fullness in the person of Jesus Christ. Revelation no longer appears simply as a body of supernatural truths contained in Scripture and taught by the Church. There is a clear movement in *Dei verbum* away from revelation as simply truths disclosed (*revelata*) to personal disclosure (*revelatio*)[43]. The basic emphasis is now placed on the personal self-communication of God to humanity in Christ. This does not neglect or diminish the new knowledge expressed in doctrine that results from this personal disclosure (n.6). It does imply, however, that this new knowledge is something consequent to the more important emphasis on the personal self-communication of God in Christ.

In more specific terms revelation, according to *Dei verbum*, is an act of God who out of the abundance of divine love communicates God's self to people through Christ for the express purpose of giving a share in the divine nature (n.2). As such revelation is Trinitarian: it is an act of God the Father, who discloses God's self through the Word Incarnate in Jesus, with a view to drawing humanity to the Divine self in the Holy Spirit.

Revelation, therefore, is a personal invitation by God out of love addressed to the individual in faith to enter into a new life of fellowship with God's self (n.2).

This revelation of God to the person takes place in history through words and deeds which have 'an inner unity' (n.2). The saving events of history are interpreted by words and at the same time these words proclaim the significance of history. Clearly revelation is more than the communication of an abstract body of truths about God. It is the experience of the personal presence of God in history imaginatively interpreted by the faith of the community. The content of God's self-revelation is available to us in the faith interpretation of the apostles in the Christian scriptures. The act of God's self-communication cannot be separated from its reception by faith in saving history. An indissoluble relationship exists between the experience of revelation and the faith interpretation of that experience. This basic unity between revelation and faith is given to us in the person of Christ found in the Scriptures and tradition.

Dei verbum brings out strongly the Christocentric character of all revelation. Jesus Christ is the personal mediator and the fullness of God's revelation (n.2). Everything that preceded the incarnation is a preparation for the Gospel of Jesus Christ (n.3). Jesus perfects revelation through his words and deeds, his death and resurrection, and the final sending of the Spirit of truth (n.4). Thus revelation is complete in Christ and we await no further public revelation before the glorious manifestation of our Lord Jesus Christ (n.4). The qualification, before the return of Christ in glory, is significant. It indicates that although revelation is at present complete in Christ there is yet another dimension of revelation which is to appear when God will be all in all at the end of time (Rev 2 1:3; Eph 1:10). The God revealed in Christ (*Deus revelatus*) is also the God who remains concealed (*Deus absconditus*) until the Second Coming of Christ in glory. This fullness of revelation in Christ does not exclude growth and development in our appropriation of the Christ-event. This takes place by listening to the Word of God that comes to us in the Scriptures, in the celebration of the sacraments, especially the Eucharist, through the teaching of the Church by the Pope and bishops and the activity of the Holy Spirit in the Christian community and the world. Thus the closure of the revelations of God in Christ is in another sense the opening of revelation in the life of the Christian community.[44] Further, the Word of God continues to address humanity through the signs of the times which must be interpreted in the light of the Gospel.[45] The universal revelation of God to people continues to take place in the world; it is discerned and interpreted through the lens of Christian revelation which is normative for the followers of Jesus crucified and risen as the Christ.

The Council decree recognises a line of continuity between universal revelation, Judaic revelation, and Christian revelation (n.3). It acknowledges different moments of revelation through created realities, the call of Abraham, the patriarchs, Moses, the prophets, and last of all through Jesus Christ the Son of God (nn.3, 4). A basic unity obtains between the revelation of God in created realities and the revelation of God in history. It is the perception of this unity that enables the Decree to overcome the dichotomy and extrinsicism that exist between natural revelation and supernatural revelation which was so prominent at Vatican I. It does this by situating all within the world created by the Word (n.3) and, therefore, graced from the very beginning of time (n.5).

Dei verbum points out that the response in faith to revelation is a response of the whole person and not just a matter of the intellect. This response is addressed 'to the truth revealed' (n.5) in the person of Christ as distinct from intellectual assent merely given to a body of truths. This faith response results from the grace of God in the world and the activity of the Holy Spirit which moves the mind and heart by drawing the individual towards God (n.5). The unity that exists between revelation and faith is thus clearly recognised in the Decree.

Lastly, it must be noted that *Dei verbum* grants a proper place to experience in the process of revelation. This was a major breakthrough in view of the fact that an appeal to experience in revelation had been outlawed in the condemnations of modernism at the beginning of the twentieth century.[46] The decree states that 'Israel came to know by experience the ways of God' (n.14) with people. The medium of God's self-revelation to humanity in the past and present is human experience.

This summary of *Dei verbum* on the nature of revelation indicates the change in focus that took place at Vatican II concerning the Church's understanding of revelation. Clearly the language, the perspectives and the priorities are different from those of Vatican I. The language of Vatican II is dynamic, experiential and personalist. The perspective is no longer dualistic but rather unified and historical.[47] The priorities are centred on the personal self-communication of God experienced in history and the fullness of that revelation embodied in Christ.

This review of thinking on the nature of revelation has emphasised throughout that revelation is about the personal communication and dialogic relationship that exists between God and the humanity in past and present history. The task of theology is to keep that divine-human exchange active and alive from the side of humanity. If the reality of the loving relationship between God and God's people is seen simply as something that can be summed up in a body of truths, then the emphasis in the Church will be simply one of safeguarding the deposit of faith. This will lead inevitably to an excessive concern with the defence of a verbal orthodoxy at the expense of a living, active faith among the people of God. Verbal orthodoxy is not enough in a world that is sensitive to language-changes, keenly aware of its own historicity and immersed in a communications revolution wherein the medium expreses the message. If, on the other hand, the loving relationship between God and humanity in revelation is seen as something that goes beyond a body of truths into the deeper realms of the interpersonal, the experiential and the historical, then the concern of the Church will be to express imaginatively that relationship in a language and practice that is in touch with people's present, personal, and historical experience of God. This can only be achieved by returning to the revelation of God in Christ, not for the sake of repeating the past, but with a view to understanding the present revelation of God through the Spirit in the Church and the world. In this way the light of Christ will be able to shine forth in a world darkened by the clouds of secularism, the excesses of material consumerism, and the emptiness of most forms of postmodernity. The decree *Dei verbum* from Vatican II challenges the Church to perform this theological task by focusing on revelation as primarily a relational and personal encounter with the reality of God in Christ. On more than one occasion the Council stated quite clearly and explicitly that the mission of the Church is above all 'to reveal the mystery of God, who is the ultimate goal of man.'[48] Closer attention to the above particular shift of emphasis at Vatican II on the dynamic nature of revelation should help to overcome some of the internal tensions in the life of the Church at present.

QUESTIONS FOR DISCUSSION

1. Discuss the relationship and difference that exists between what some call general revelation and particular revelation, and others refer to as cosmic revelation and historical revelation, in Christ

2. In what way does the teaching of the Second Vatican Council on Revelation go beyond the classical presentation of Revelation in the scholastic manuals and complement the perspectives of the first Vatican Council

3. Explain what it means to say that Revelation is not available for detached, clinical inspection but only makes sense through a process of personal faith participation which is ignited by the vast array of human experiences of creation and history that people under go in the journey of life.

Recommended Readings

Articles:

- Dulles, Avery, 'Faith and Revelation', *Systematic Theology: Roman Catholic Perspectives,* vol.I, edited by Francis S. Fiorenza and John P. Galvin, Minneapolis: Fortress Press, 1991.
- O'Hara Graff, Ann, 'Ecclesial Discernment: Women's Voices, New Voices, and the Revelatory Process, *Women and Theology,* edited by Mary Ann Hinsdale and Phillis H. Kaminski, New York: Orbis Books, 1995.
- Daly, Gabriel, 'Revelation in the Theology of the Roman Catholic Church', *Divine Revelation,* edited by Paul Avis, London: DLT, 1997.

- Leahy, Brendan, 'Revelation and Faith', *Evangelisation for the Third Millennium,* T. Norris and M. Hogan (eds.) Dublin: Veritas, 1997,
- Murray, Robert, 'Vatican II and the Bible', *Downside Review,* January 2003: 14-25.

Books:
- Dulles, Avery, *Models of Revelation,* New York: Doubleday, 1983
- Haught, John F., *Mystery and Promise: A Theology of Revelation,* Minnesota: M. Glazier/Liturgical Press, 1993
- O'Collins, Gerard, *Retrieving Fundamental Theology,* New York: Paulist Press, 1993

3

THE ACTIVITY OF FAITH

Faith is answered revelation. Accepted revelation is faith. Faith is revelation arrived at its goal. ... The analyses of faith in the human realm point out that personal ... self-communication is an act of the spirit and of freedom, above all, an act of love and truth. Persons can close themselves off, keep silent, or dissemble. Accordingly, the faith that is co-ordinated to the revelation of a person is an act of respect, honour, and high esteem (Heinrich Fries)[1]

The reality of faith is not simply a world to itself alone, separate from the world of secular experience, if only because this faith raises quite concrete claims and demands which must be fulfilled in the concrete world of secular experience and activity, in moral life and in the ecclesial society, which is a very concrete reality of everyday existence (Karl Rahner)[2]

T he theology of faith is a foundational issue. The response in faith which the believer addresses to God's revelation in the cosmos and history is the basis of theology. In many respects faith is the centre of gravity around which everything else in theology revolves. As a result, the way in which we understand faith will determine the way we do theology and it will also shape the character of Christian consciousness. For example, if we see faith as an intellectual assent to a series of propositions, then theology will be driven to defend these statements of faith. If, on the other hand, we understand faith as a relational response of the whole person to the mystery of God co-present in human experience, then theology will appear as an exploration of human experience in a way that illuminates the active, omnipresent mystery of God in general and special revelation.

In trying to elaborate a theology of faith, attention must be given to the context in which questions of faith arise. That context includes such diverse developments in the twentieth century as the collapse of classical culture which has given birth to the rise of historical consciousness,[3] the primacy of the appeal to experience in theology, the development of a personalist understanding of revelation, the existence of doctrinal pluralism, the impact of science on our understanding of the world and the healthy secularisation that follows from this. At the same time a contemporary theology of faith must seek to avoid the perennial pitfalls of fundamentalism, fideism, rationalism, deism, pantheism and the different forms of secularist, positivist (biblical and doctrinal), and relativist reductionism that exists in regard to the transcendent dimension of Christian faith.

The purpose of this chapter is not to address formally these challenges and dangers. Instead it will attempt more modestly to construct a framework for understanding the nature and structure of Christian faith that is alive to these developments and pitfalls. It will do this by outlining the universal character of faith, discussing the relationship that exists between faith and belief, commenting on the unity that obtains between grace and faith, and finally by pointing the way forward for the future of faith.

The Universal Character of Faith

Until recently the concept of faith was understood primarily as a religious category. Faith was seen as something only religious people have. Indeed for too long people were divided into two distinct groups depending on whether they had faith or not. We still refer too easily to believers and non-believers as if believers had faith and non-believers were those who had no faith. This way of thinking and classifying people is no longer acceptable. Faith is by no means an exclusively religious category; it can also be found among non-religious people.

Recent studies have shown that faith in fact is an element that belongs intrinsically and universally to the human condition. One of the interesting things about these studies is that they have come out of quite different stables of research. On the one hand those engaged in the cross-cultural study of religion point out that faith is a constitutive dimension of the person[4] and that to be human is to have faith.[5] According to Wilfred Cantwell Smith, faith is generally a human quality.[6] Further, the thesis that faith is constitutive of the individual, according to Pannikar, 'claims to be as valid for a Buddhist as for one who calls himself an atheist'.[7] On the other hand, James Fowler, who has been working on the question of faith-development by using the foundational frameworks of Piaget and Kohlberg on moral development, has come up with the claim that faith is 'a human universal, a feature of living, acting, and self-understanding, of all human beings whether or not they would claim to be 'religious' in any traditional way'.[8] For Fowler, faith is a 'structuring activity'[9] brought to bear on our many experiences, activities and modes of understanding. Faith gives 'form to our affirmations about experience taken as a whole' in a way that relates them to a 'unifying centre of meaning and value'.[10] A similar point of view on the nature of faith is put forward by David Tracy who points out:

> The authentic person is committed above all else to the full affirmation of the ultimate significance of our lives in this world. Such a fundamental commitment may be described as a faith. [11]

This basic faith addressed to the worthwhileness of human existence is shared by the secular person and the Christian person alike.

In the light of these studies it must be stated clearly that faith is fundamentally a human quality that belongs to all people. For the sake of convenience, we shall refer to this kind of faith as 'primordial faith' to distinguish it from the more explicit form of faith we will call 'religious faith'. Primordial faith is a quality that belongs as much to secular forms of human interaction as it does to religious traditions. Atheists and humanists are not people who live without faith; rather they are people whose faith does not consciously contain a formal religious component.[12] The real issue today about faith is not whether one has faith but rather what particular kind of faith one has. As John Shea points out, the 'effort to make faith valuable by making it rare is misguided. Faith is as common and unavoidable as air'.[13] How then are we to understand human primordial faith?

Primordial faith is an attitude of trust and confidence and acceptance that is brought to bear on the value and worthwhileness of human existence. This attitude shapes the way we filter our experiences of persons, events and community. Faith enables people to live in community. The details of this attitude can vary enormously from individual to individual. The basis (*ratio*) of this faith outlook is not something that is immediately self-evident or demonstrable, nor is it a conclusion that comes directly from logic or formal inference. Faith is a way of life: a way of being and behaving in the world that is informed by such complex factors as the personal experience of existence, education, community and tradition. Primordial faith is the underlying presupposition of existence in the world. Thus the preface to a study of faith in the late 1970s begins:

> Anyone not about to kill himself lives by faith. It is what keeps us going ... Faith carries us forward. It enables us to exist ... Faith is a *sine qua non* of life, a primal force.[14]

The dictum *crede ut intelligas* – believe so that you may understand – has been claimed rather exclusively by the Christian faith. It figures prominently in the writings of Augustine and Aquinas. However, the saying is much older than Christianity. One form exists in the Old Testament in Isaiah 7:9:

> If you do not believe you will not exist.

Another form is found in Aristotle:

Whoever wishes to understand must believe.[15]

The interpretation of these texts in the past has been rather intellectualist. This reflects the great concern within the Christian tradition about the relationship that exists between faith and intellectual freedom as well as the tendency to define the individual in rationalist terms. An equally valid interpretation, however, would be an existentialist one which would imply that if you want to exist, to be authentically with others, then you must have some kind of faith. In other words, some form of faith is necessary and essential to the process of being fully human.[16]

What it is precisely that we believe in is, of course, the central issue in any discussion of faith. What is it in life that keeps us going, that gives meaning to our experience, coherence and unity to existence, that sustains us through history, and that ultimately enables us 'to become' what we are and 'to be' what we become? When we begin to answer these questions we begin to translate faith into belief, though this does not mean, as we shall presently see, that faith is simply a matter of belief. There are many ways of answering these questions and so there are many beliefs or, as one might say, many forms of faith. For instance, the Marxist organises experience around belief in historical progress through the class struggle whereas the Christian centres the meaning of existence in the person of Jesus as the revelation of God. This does not mean that the only difference between primordial and religious faith is simply a matter of beliefs.

Certainly, beliefs clearly distinguish religious faith from primordial faith. Not only beliefs, however, but the precise nature of the faith involved seems to distinguish religious faith from primordial faith. To be sure, primordial faith and religious faith have many points in common. At the same time, there does appear to be a fundamental difference in terms of faith itself. Surely a difference in faith exists at least at the level of consciousness, in virtue of the fact that in one case faith is normally referred to a transcendent reality whereas in the other case faith is centred exclusively on reality as confined to this world. Furthermore, it is hardly sufficient to suggest that religious faith is simply the representation of the individual's basic human faith in existence.[17] This seems to imply that there is no significant difference between primordial and religious faith. Faith, though universal, cannot be flattened out into sameness for everybody. There is a difference, perhaps even a cut-off point, between primordial faith and religious faith. This difference is more than beliefs; it is also, we suggest, the nature of religious faith itself. Religious faith deepens, extends, and transforms primordial faith. There is a degree of continuity as well as discontinuity between primordial faith and religious faith.

The element of discontinuity will become more apparent in the course of this chapter. For the moment we wish to highlight the continuity that exists between primordial and religious faith. Faith is a fundamental human quality, it is universal, it is constitutive of the human condition, it enables the individual to realise personhood in community. The corollary to this, of course, is that faith is not something exceptional nor is it some kind of optional extra. As one author sums up 'The standard human being is a human being of faith.'[18] The complex relationship between primordial, basic faith and religious faith could be represented, crudely speaking, in the following diagram:

KINDS OF FAITH

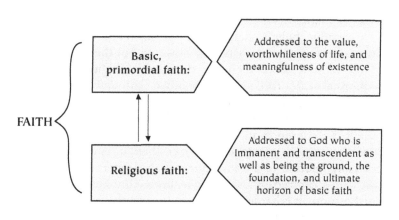

THE EXPERIENCE OF GOD

In recognising the universal quality of faith the above authors have provided fundamental theology with an important apologetical point of departure for discussing religious faith and dialoguing with those who profess to be non-religious. To appreciate the uniqueness of religious faith, and in particular Christian faith, we must say something about the distinction and relationship that exists between faith and belief.

The Act of Faith and Belief

One of the most muddled areas of contemporary theology is the relationship and distinction that exists between faith and what we call belief. This was not always the case within Christianity. In fact the confusion that reigns at present is a peculiarly modern problem. We suggest that this confusion is responsible in no small part for many of the current problems that exist in the area of faith.

Within the Christian tradition a close relationship always existed between faith and belief. Faith was understood as a personal act of surrender addressed to God. The act of faith assumed a certain imaginative framework and took for granted basic theoretical presuppositions. These latter were regarded as the content of faith. Faith and its presuppositions, though related, were distinct. Faith was not identified simply with its imaginative framework. Yet faith without some presuppositions was regarded as empty.

In recent times, however, some confusion has arisen between faith and belief. For many, faith has become identified with belief while at the same time belief itself has come to mean the underlying presuppositions of faith. As a result, faith is reduced at times to the acceptance of a series of basic propositions.

Some of this confusion is semantic and some of it is simply bad theology. A short review of the history of the meaning of faith in Christianity should help to disentangle some of the knots that have been tied between faith and belief.[19]

In the New Testament the same root word is used for both the noun 'faith' and the verb 'to make the act of faith': *pistis* and *pisteuo*. The Greek verb *pisteuo*, used in the New Testament for the act of faith, means to commit, to trust, to pledge, to dedicate oneself; it does not mean belief in the modern sense of subscribing to a series of propositions. The act of faith in the New Testament is a highly personal and existential act addressed to God. It also includes a cognitive component, not in terms of propositions but in terms of recognising and perceiving the truth as well as appropriating that truth.[20] The curious thing about the New Testament is that there are very few references to belief in the modern sense, whereas most of the references to faith are about the personal and practical activity of turning to God in Christ.[21]

This activity of faith in the New Testament was translated into Latin by the verb *credo* (I believe), and the noun used was *fides* (faith). The verb 'I believe'/*credo* in the early Church did not signify a theoretical activity of the mind, nor did it in any sense refer to the acceptance of a series of propositions. The verb 'I believe'/*credo* is a compound of the noun *cor (cordis)*, meaning heart, and the verb *do*, to put, to place, to set, which is distinct from though related to the other verb *do (dare)*, to give. Thus the root meaning of 'I believe'/credo is 'I set my heart on', 'I give my heart to'. Taken in the context of the New Testament and used in association with baptism and the early creeds, 'I believe'/*credo* meant 'I hereby commit myself', 'I pledge myself'.[22] 'I believe'/*credo*, in the context of baptism, was about pledging oneself to Christ in terms of a movement from darkness to illumination, a passage from a life of sinfulness to a life of grace, a change from involvement in one order to a committed involvement in the new order of creation in Christ. When used in reference to the early creeds, 'I believe'/*credo* contrary to popular understanding, was not primarily addressed to propositional statements. Instead 'I believe'/*credo*, was about the activity of becoming involved and engaged with the God revealed in Jesus Christ. The practical and performative character of this act of faith in baptism is brought out in the response 'I do'.

We are not suggesting here that 'I believe'/*credo* in the early Church did not involve accepting an imaginative framework, a conceptual outlook, and theoretical presuppositions. 'I believe'/*credo* did include these, not as the primary object of faith but as the context. Further, these elements were not normally referred to by the early Church in terms of belief. Rather,

THE EXPERIENCE OF GOD

believing in the early Church signified the activity of personal commitment and allegiance to God in Christ. The 'I believe' / *credo* of the early Church in reference to baptism and the creeds was a performative act of giving oneself over completely to the Christian God.

Thus it is quite clear that Christian faith in the early Church was not primarily about the acceptance of certain theoretical positions that had implications about daily living. Instead, Christian faith was a personal and practical way of living, centred in Christ Jesus that entailed content and theoretical implications.

This distinction between faith in God through Christ and the theological framework supporting that personal act of faith was developed formally by the Scholastics. They distinguished between the personal act of faith and the content of faith, between what some called the reality (*res*) of faith and the words (*verba*) communicating that reality, between what others called belief in (*fides qua*) and belief about (*fides quae*). St Thomas Aquinas reminds us forcefully:

> The act of the believer does not terminate with the proposition but in the reality (behind the proposition).[23]

In a similar vein Aquinas continues:

> Anyone who believes (i.e. makes the act of faith) gives assent to someone's saying, and so in any form of belief it is the person to whose saying assent is given who is of primary importance, whereas the beliefs through which we sent assent to the person are, so to speak, secondary.[24]

For Aquinas the goal of faith is the living reality of God and the means to this are the different expressions of faith (*sacra doctrina*). Aquinas is quite insistent that beliefs, the content of faith, are significant 'only insofar as they have some reference to God i.e., as they are the workings of God that help human beings in striving toward joyous rest in God.'[25]

This clear distinction and relationship between the act of faith and the content of faith (beliefs in the modern sense) continued more or less as outlined until the seventeenth century. In the seventeenth century and the eighteenth century the content of faith began to move away from the act of faith, becoming independent and detached from the act of faith. Believing in God became synonymous with believing that God... This development, or more accurately distortion, hardened in the nineteenth century with the result that in the twentieth century the act of faith, in many instances, had become identified with the content of faith.[26]

During the twentieth century an even more serious distortion has arisen. Beliefs have come to be associated, at least in the popular mind, with that which is regarded as mere opinion, the uncertain and at times doubtful.[27]

Looking back on this brief survey we discover that the meaning of belief has undergone serious changes. For some sixteen hundred years belief referred to the personal and practical act of commitment of oneself to God in Christ with all one's heart and with all one's mind. Then belief/believing began to be associated in the seventeenth century onward with assent to theoretical expressions of faith. In the latter half of the twentieth century belief/believing is taken by some to mean subscribing to things about which we are not certain. In effect, belief has taken over from faith with the following unhappy threefold result: faith appears as something propositional rather than personal, faith comes across as the passive acceptance of truths without any personal engagement, and faith seems to be about that which is intellectually shaky and dubious.

In the light of this distortion of faith by belief it is imperative to recover and restate the classical understanding of faith. This becomes all the more urgent in the twenty-first century in which we hear so much talk about the existence of a so-called crisis of faith. Such talk about a crisis of faith ought to be more nuanced. Is it a crisis of faith in the proper sense of the word 'faith' or is it a crisis in the theoretical expression of faith (i.e. a crisis of belief), or is it perhaps a protest by people against the inflation of belief at the expense of the more important factor of personal faith? While we cannot answer these questions here, we must at least establish the proper meaning and primacy of the personal act of faith in relation to belief.

The personal act of faith, according to Aquinas, is directed to 'primal truth', in modern language absolute truth and/or ultimate reality, which is identified with God[28]. Faith is a love of truth, a personal dedication to truth, and a practical living out of life according to the truth. Faith is insight into the truth of God followed by a personal response to that insight which affects daily living. There is a difference in knowing something is true and actually participating in that perception of truth. Faith is a personal participation at all levels of life in the truth of God. Faith is also a recognition of God that alters lifestyles. Faith, therefore, is primarily a practical affair, especially in its effects, rather than a purely theoretical stance.[29]

Faith is a decision to enter into a personal relationship with God. This relationship is one of love, trust, and confidence addressed to God as personal. More accurately, faith is, as Paul Tillich liked to point out, 'the acceptance of being accepted by God.' Faith is the acknowledgement and affirmation of a relationship with God, initiated by God in the act of creation by bringing us into existence in the first instance. Faith is also an act of surrender to God, a placing of one's heart and one's affections in God. Faith is, therefore, an act of the whole person involving intellect and will as well as emotions, feelings and imagination.

Faith is an act that changes the individual; it brings about a conversion, a conversion that touches the whole outlook, attitude and imagination of the individual. Thus, the act of faith structures human experience, feelings, and activities around God as the transcendent Centre of our lives. Faith allows this personal transcendent Centre to give unity, meaning and identity to human existence. Faith, therefore, is the experience of living before, in, and around the presence of God.

The act of faith is always addressed to God, not as a scientific formula but as a living personal reality that is active in creation, history and the lives of people. Faith is addressed to God as the origin and goal, or better, in the words of Rahner, 'the whence and whither' of authentic experiences of self-transcendence. Faith, from beginning to end, is theocentric, being addressed to God as incomprehensible and ineffable.

For the Christian, faith is addressed to the truth of God revealed in Christ. Christian faith is a personal relationship with God as Father through Christ in the Holy Spirit. Christian faith is centred in the person of Jesus as the Son of God incarnate. Christian faith, therefore, is informed by Jesus as the decisive and definitive revelation of God to the world. Christian faith is a personal commitment to Christ as the centre of creation, the source of unity among his disciples and the hope of humanity. For Christian faith, Jesus Christ represents what the human person is called to be and shows the way to the realisation of full humanity (*vere homo*). At the same time Jesus discloses the true face of God to the world and opens up the truth that is God (*vere Deus*). Lastly, Christian faith recognises the Christian community as the bearer and Sacrament of Christ in the world today.

As we begin to express the basic features of Christian faith we immediately become involved in outlining the content of faith. This highlights the fact that faith is vague and indeterminate without beliefs. Faith needs beliefs, but faith is not identifiable with beliefs. Beliefs mediate faith, conceptualise faith and communicate faith. Beliefs, however, do not give us a literal or one-to-one account of the formal 'object' of faith. Beliefs are the human expression of our understanding of the mystery of God and are, to that extent, subjective, that is, they come from the side of humanity and are not given objectively from above.[30] In contrast, faith can be said to be objective in the sense that it is directed to the transcendent reality of God. Beliefs are historical and, therefore, they reflect the cultural circumstances of their original definition. As historical, beliefs are also plural and diverse, whereas faith, which perceives truth in the midst of plurality, is one and unifying.

It should now be clear that faith expresses itself in beliefs, is sustained by beliefs, depends on beliefs, but is not reducible to beliefs. There is no such thing as pure or 'neat' faith; faith does not exist without beliefs. Faith exists embedded in beliefs, yet the beliefs are only a partial expression of the fullness of divine truth to which faith is committed. For this reason faith always goes beyond the historicity and plurality of beliefs. Faith realises in humility and obedience that there is always more to the truth of

God than that contained in particular and historical accounts of that truth. Beliefs are a means to faith. There is more in faith than beliefs can express. No amount of adding up of beliefs can ever equal faith. So it must be acknowledged that beliefs are subordinate to and answerable to the transcendent reality of God.[31] To ignore these limitations of beliefs would be to diminish the primacy of faith over belief and to move rather close to a form of doctrinal positivism.

However, in spite of these limitations that attach to belief, it must be pointed out that it is impossible to suspend all beliefs and continue to profess faith in God revealed through Christ. It is logically inconsistent and indeed theologically impossible to claim, for example, 'I accept the person of Jesus but I do not believe his teachings.' Faith in Christ carries with it a commitment to the teachings of Christ. Equally, it is unacceptable to claim, 'I pledge myself to the Church of Christ but I do not take its teaching seriously.' This kind of doublethink errs by severing the indissoluble relationship that exists between the act of faith and the content of faith. Once these two aspects of faith are separated, then the truth of faith itself is disturbed. This separation of faith and belief seems to forget that it is only in and through the message that we meet the Messenger and that it is only as a result of the gifts that we recognise the Giver. To try to find faith by isolating it from belief is a little like trying to find the onion by peeling away the skin. There is always Someone loved and valued and trusted in the act of Faith. It is essential to be able to describe in meaningful terms that Someone who is loved, valued and trusted. This is precisely the role that belief plays.

The content of the act of faith is usually summed up in terms of creed, code and cult, or what is more technically termed *orthodoxy, orthopoiesis* and *orthopraxis*.[32] The creed, or orthodoxy, embraces the doctrinal content of the act of faith. The horizon of orthodoxy tends to be intellectual and the goal is the expression of the Truth of faith. Obviously faith could not survive without some intellectual content. On the other hand, orthodoxy by no means contains the totality of faith.

There is also the important element of code or *orthopoiesis.* This aspect concerns the moral implications of the act of faith. It spells out the responsibilities and obligations that follow from the personal act of faith. *Orthopoiesis* is about moral deportment and it is usually summed up in terms of commandments. Again, this dimension of faith should not be identified with the entirety of the act of faith.

The third element, cult or, better, orthopraxis, is crucial to the act of faith. Orthopraxis must be distinguished from orthodoxy and *orthopoiesis*. Orthodoxy is about knowing the Truth and *orthopoiesis* is about doing good in terms of an activity addressed to an object without necessarily effecting any real change. In contrast, orthopraxis is about doing the truth in a way that changes the subject and the recipient. In particular, orthopraxis should not be seen as simply the application of theory to practice. Rather, orthopraxis is the critical correlation of theory and practice whereby each influences and transforms the other. Orthopraxis embraces the performance of a transforming activity in the world, such as action for justice, in the name of the kingdom of God as well as the transforming activities of prayer and worship. Liturgy as a part of orthopraxis entails change and conversion not only in the subject but also, properly speaking, in the social and political realms. Good liturgy will always issue in some kind of transforming activity on behalf of the poor and the needy in the community. This is sometimes lost sight of due to the ease and frequency with which we engage in liturgical celebration. Is it not the case that the whole thrust of the Judaeo-Christian prophetic tradition is a plea for connecting liturgy and justice? Worship without the praxis of justice is the object of critical protest in the Bible (Am 5:21-25; Is 1:13ff; 58:6ff; Mt 9:13; 5:23-25).

In addition, the orthopraxis of prayer is essential to the life of faith; prayer sustains faith in existence and provides the ambience for developing faith. A close correspondence obtains between the life of faith and the practice of prayer. Faith issues in prayer and prayer transforms faith.

All three elements are integral to a proper appreciation of Christian faith. Faith, in the Christian tradition, has always been seen as necessary for salvation, and as a result our understanding of faith has shaped our perception of salvation. For example, when the element of orthodoxy predominated, then salvation was understood as some kind of intellectual vision; when orthopoiesis was emphasised, salvation appeared as a reward for doing good. Today with the emphasis on orthopraxis, which seems to accord more faithfully with the Gospel of Jesus Christ, salvation is understood in terms of change and transformation summed up in the central communitarian New Testament symbols of resurrection, new creation, and the advent of the kingdom of God.

At the risk of being misunderstood we might sum up the relationship between faith and belief in the following way:

> Faith unites, beliefs divide;
> Beliefs are diverse, faith is one;
> Faith is objective, beliefs subjective;
> Beliefs are symbolic, faith is transcendent;
> Faith is personal, beliefs propositional;
> Beliefs are historical, faith is permanent;
> Faith is God-given, beliefs community-made;
> Beliefs are theoretical, faith is practical.

The differentiated unity that exists between the personal act of faith and the content of faith can be represented, at least symbolically, in the diagram on p.88.

The Bond Between Grace and Faith

Obviously one of the most important issues facing any theology of faith today is the question: How does the individual come to make the act of faith? An immediate answer to this question might suggest that the person comes to faith by accepting a series of beliefs. While it is true that the act of faith does involve adherence to certain beliefs, it should be clear by now that there is more to faith than beliefs and that differences between primordial and religious faith as already implied, are more than simply differences in belief. The difference between religious faith and primordial faith lies ultimately in the nature of the act of religious faith.

The act of religious faith is, as we have just seen, addressed to the mystery of God. As such the 'object' of religious faith is

THE CHARACTERISTICS OF CHRISTIAN FAITH

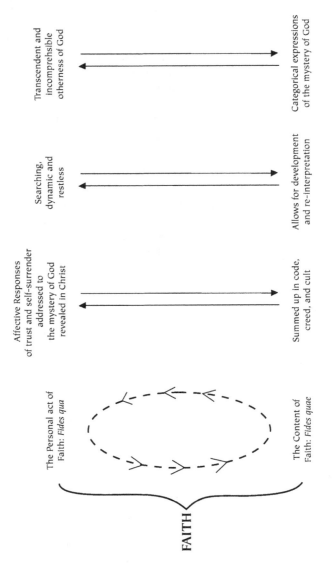

The Personal act of
Faith: *Fides qua*

Affective Responses
of trust and self-surrender
addressed to
the mystery of God
revealed in Christ

Searching,
dynamic and
restless

Transcendent and
incomprehsible
otherness of God

The Content of
Faith: *Fides quae*

Summed up in code,
creed, and cult

Allows for development
and re-interpretation

Categorical expressions
of the mystery of God

FAITH

transcendent and transcendental. It is transcendent insofar as the intentionality of the act of faith goes beyond all finite realities in the world. It is transcendental in the sense that the act of faith exceeds adequate representation in human formulas. Further, performing the act of faith is such that it brings about a fundamental conversion in the life of the individual which is usually summed up in terms of religious, moral and intellectual change as well as, from the Christian point of view, containing a specifically Christian and ecclesial dimension. We have already seen something about the specifically Christian dimension of faith. As for the ecclesial aspect, suffice it to say here that it consists in holding that individual Christian faith can only exist in relation to and contact with the community of faith we call the Church. In addition, the performance of the act of religious faith is something unique and specific to the influence of the 'object' of faith itself upon the individual. This final point, differentiating religious faith from human faith, needs to be elaborated upon because of its importance.

It has always been held by the Christian tradition that the act of faith is brought about by the grace of God. The classic texts in Scripture are: 'No one can come to me unless the Father draws him' (Jn 6:44); 'We love because God loved us first' (1 Jn 4:19); 'For by grace you have been saved through faith; and this is not your own doing, it is the gift of God' (Eph 2:8). All agree that faith is a gift from God, but how, and in what sense, it is a gift from God is a matter of some theological discussion. How does God draw the individual in faith to God's self? What kind of divine action is involved in the dynamics of religious faith. Is this divine action a grace given to some and withheld from others?

In response to these very reasonable questions it must be pointed out that contemporary theology sees the grace of God in the world as a universal reality.[33] We live in a world of grace. Every human being comes into the world graced by God. Every individual is called by God to communion with God in this life and in eternity. One of the most significant and far-reaching advances of Vatican II was the formal recognition of this basic theological position.[34] A similar perspective can be found among the early Fathers of the Church; they spoke about the universal grace of

God in the world as 'first grace' which is completed by the 'second grace' of God in Christ.[35]

It was Aquinas, however, who worked out a developed theology of the relationship that exists between the universal grace of God and the act of faith. Aquinas distinguished between interior grace and exterior grace,[36] between the inner invitation given to all and the outer expression of that contained in Christian revelation. According to Aquinas there exists in the heart (*in affectione*) an 'inner instinct which impels and moves us to believe.'[37] The individual 'is prompted to believe ... by an inner instinct from God drawing him to belief.'[38] It is this inner instinct of faith that disposes the human person to make the act of faith. It enables the individual to recognise and respond to the exterior grace of God's revelation in Christ. The personal act of faith comes into being as a result of the correspondence that exists between the inner grace of faith and the exterior grace of God in Christ.

This graced orientation of humanity manifests itself in a thousand different ways. Some speak about the restlessness of the human heart (Augustine) while others point to the reasons of the heart which reason cannot reason (Pascal). During the twentieth century this interior disposition of grace has been described as the dynamism of the will (Blondel), the natural desire for God (de Lubac), the supernatural existential (Rahner) and the unrestricted desire to know and love (Lonergan). These particular descriptions of the nature of the human person are an expression of and testimony to the universal grace of God that has touched and affected every individual in the world.

This interior disposition of grace in the person is activated in and through the multiplicity of experiences the individual undergoes. Some of the more outstanding experiences in this regard would include the experience of the contingency of existence,[39] the positive and negative limit situations we encounter in life,[40] the dynamic drive toward self-transcendence,[41] and our daily contact with good and evil in the world. These fundamental experiences, and others too numerous to list, spark off the first movements of the act of faith. They stir up within the individual an openness and readiness to hear the gracious Word

THE EXPERIENCE OF GOD

of God. It is important to note here that this inner instinct, this underlying orientation, this hunger of the human heart for God, is not faith as such. Of itself this interior grace of faith is incomplete. It needs the outer Word of God contained in the Gospel of Jesus Christ to bring it to completion. In this sense faith comes from hearing (*ex auditiu,* Rom 10:17). The interior movements of the instinct of faith provide a point of entry for the exterior grace of the Word of God which brings about the act of faith. Thus Rahner writes:

> The grace of God has always been there ... ahead of our preaching ... Our preaching is not really an indoctrination with something alien from outside but the awakening of something within, as yet not understood but nevertheless really present.[42]

Greater attention should be given to these initial movements of the human spirit by teasing out the implications of the multiple experiences that people undergo. This zeroing-in on the inner dynamism of human experience should not be construed as a reductionism of faith; rather it should be seen as an essential preparation for the Gospel (*preparatio evangelica*). It is only by attending to these experiences inspired by grace that we will be able to announce meaningfully the Word of God to contemporary women and men.

The thesis that humanity is graced from the beginning is based ultimately on the doctrine of creation. The act of creation by God is such that the individual comes into the world in one particular way rather than another. This particular way is the way of a graced nature. People are born into the world in the warmth of God's love which never leaves them. That love of God directs humanity in a particular way, somewhat like a magnet drawing pieces of iron unto itself. This particular understanding of the act of creation is confirmed by the special revelation of the universal saving will of God in Christ. God wills all to be saved in Christ (1 Tim 4:10). This original plan of God does have an effect on the historical condition of human nature. It alters the very nature of the individual. It means that there is in every human being an effect which corresponds to the original design of God's plan. This effect may be described as 'first grace' (the Fathers), the inner instinct of faith (Aquinas), the supernatural existential (Rahner), the underlying orientation of every individual toward God. What this view of creation implies in particular is that the grace of faith, this interior instinct of the individual for God, is not some occasional impulse that comes and goes in the life of the individual, nor is it something that is merely intermittent. Rather, the grace of faith, which draws the human spirit to God in the act of faith, is the abiding condition of human freedom. From beginning to end, the individual is a radical reference to God raised up by grace.[43]

This act of religious faith begins with God and ends in God. The act of faith is effected by God, and it is this perhaps more than anything else that distinguishes religious faith from primordial faith.[44] The act of religious faith is inspired by 'first grace' and sustained in existence by 'second grace'. The flowering forth of these graces requires the full and free cooperation of each individual. The act of religious faith is one of the ways that the individual responds to these God-given graces. It is an act that changes the horizon and consciousness of the individual to such a degree that it is possible to hold that there is a basic difference between primordial faith and religious faith, a difference in outlook, attitude, imagination and praxis.

The Future of Faith

We have seen that faith expresses itself in beliefs and that faith cannot exist without belief. Beliefs, however, are not an end in themselves. Their primary purpose is to bring us to a deeper understanding of the inexhaustible and ineffable mystery that is God. The validity of beliefs in the future will have to be judged more in accordance with the Thomistic criterion of being able to open up the mystery of God and at the same time relate the individual to that mystery.[45]

At the present time there exists a certain degree of tension between faith and belief in different Christian communities of faith. Some tension is inevitable and even desirable in view of the particular role that beliefs play in the service of faith. Beliefs are a human attempt to express the inexpressible and to describe the ineffable in finite, historical, and cultural terms. We live in a world of change. The twentieth century is an era that has undergone colossal cultural change. Bernard Lonergan points out:

> The breakdown of classical culture and ... the manifest comprehensiveness of modern culture confront Catholic philosophy and Catholic theology with the gravest problems, impose upon them mountainous tasks, invite them to Herculean labors.[46]

This cultural change affects radically the way we formulate beliefs. The continued formulation of beliefs in a language and a culture that belong to another age can become an obstacle to belief and ultimately to faith itself. For example, reliance on a double-decker cosmology, the use of a non-historical perspective, the employment of a dualistic anthropology, and adherence to outmoded philosophical categories simply for the sake of repeating the past, when it comes to expressing faith, will have, and is having, an alienating effect on the present generation of Christian believers. Cultural change is a fact of life and is set to continue, perhaps even more dramatically, in the twenty-first century. No amount of complaining will make it go away or reduce it. If anything the pace of change will continue to be felt in the twenty-first century, especially with the advent of new technologies, religious pluralism, post-modern culture, and globalisation. What is important, however, from the point of view of faith is that we recognise and accept the need for belief to keep pace with such cultural changes.

Another reason for the existence of this tension between faith and belief today is the absence of any felt relationship between the formulas of faith and contemporary experience. Yet, as we have seen, the act of faith is animated by the dynamic orientation of human experiences. Once belief loses contact with experience it becomes an empty formula to be simply repeated without any personal meaning. This implies that beliefs must be seen to be related to, and saying something about, contemporary experience without however being reduced simply to the level of human experience. A mutually critical correlation between the formulas of faith and human experience must be continually worked out. We must accept that particular expressions of belief are open to revision, reinterpretation, and re-imagination in the service of a living faith in God.

These tensions between faith and belief can be viewed differently. On the one hand, they can be seen as a healthy sign of the vitality of faith – a faith that is permanently seeking further elucidation. New expressions of belief are essential to a living faith. Controversy about belief should be seen, in many instances, as a genuine attempt to keep belief in tune with the dynamics of living faith. To this extent there must exist a place within the community of faith for the free and responsible exploration of the dialectic that exists between faith and belief. Without this creative tension between faith and belief, there is always the danger that faith itself will die and belief become redundant. On the other hand, there comes a stage when the crisis of belief can become a crisis of faith. This occurs when faith is tied to particular expressions and the imaginative exploration of new formulas in the name of faith is excluded. When this happens, a situation of apathy and indifference takes over wherein the transcendent dimension of faith becomes marginal and ineffectual in the lives of people. Further, the difference between religious faith and primordial faith becomes blurred, not only at the level of belief, but also at the level of the personal act of faith itself.

One of the most serious threats facing faith today is the presence of a growing apathy and indifference toward faith. Such a situation may well be more serious than the existence of formal atheism. Formal atheism, at least, however regrettable, is a worked-out position in which the search for truth is still in motion. As long as people are searching for the truth, dialogue and discussion can take place. However, with apathy and indifference the quest for truth has died. When this happens the community of faith must engage in a serious process of self-criticism and self-analysis. The question must be faced why there is indifference to that which is universal, human and in keeping with humanity's deepest aspirations. Does the problem lie with the indifferent, or is it perhaps with that which the indifferent are being invited to respond to by the community of faith and the mediations of faith in that community? This particular question becomes all the more acute when we bear in mind that every individual has, as we have seen, a natural capacity for God, that all have been graced by God *ab initio* with a corresponding real effect in their hearts, and that God is already revealed to the world in the person of Jesus of Nazareth. Is it possible, perhaps, that the indifferent have only been offered beliefs when it was faith they were searching for? Have we replaced the living, dynamic personal reality of God by a series of cold, complex conceptualisations? Have we given people stones when they asked for bread? One way of overcoming these dangers is by carefully distinguishing (not separating) faith from belief and by spelling out the creative relationship that exists between them both.[47]

Furthermore, if we are to cope with the necessary and inevitable tensions that exist between faith and belief, then more attention in the future will have to be given to the existence of a 'hierarchy of truths' within Christianity, the recognition of some form of legitimate pluralism in the expression of faith, and the presence of different 'stages of faith' in the lives of people.

The Second Vatican Council, and subsequent Church documents, acknowledge that there exists within Catholicism a 'hierarchy of truths'.[48] This means that some beliefs are more important than others. Obviously there are some truths that hold a less prominent position when it comes to expressing the core of Christian faith. Some kind of differentiation must be made in regard to the basic beliefs of Christianity. Until this is done more formally than heretofore little progress will be made in regard to developing faith and Christian unity. There are certain basic beliefs that make up the centre of Christian faith without which Christian faith would no longer be Christian faith.[49]

This call to recognise the existence of a hierarchy of truths in Christian faith should not be interpreted as a call to list a number of truths which in some way could add up to faith. To the contrary, it is a call to move from a quantitative understanding of faith to a qualitative appreciation of faith. There was a tendency in pre-Vatican II times to stress quantitatively all Christian beliefs as if they were of equal qualitative importance in God's plan of salvation. As a result a serious confusion arose between the means of salvation, such as Church, sacraments and office, and the goal of salvation which is eternal life in God through Christ. This confusion can be overcome by making

> ... a clear distinction between *credere in Deum*, in *Jesum Christum, in Spiritum Sanctum* on the one hand and *credere Ecclesiam* on the other. The Church and all that accompanies it, particularly the sacraments and offices, are believed in a different way from God, who acts in Jesus Christ through the Holy Spirit for salvation. It is to God alone that faith is directly related, and it is God who forms the real content of that faith. The Church together with its sacraments and offices is only a means of salvation, and faith is related to it to the extent that it mediates salvation and makes it present. The Christian therefore does not believe in the Church – or the Pope, for example – in the same way that he believes in God. The means of salvation have to be seen as ways in which salvation is mediated, and if they are no longer satisfactorily performing this function, they should be criticised.[50]

The need to recognise some degree of pluralism in the expression of faith follows from the fact that the unity of truth has many faces and that beliefs are culturally conditioned. Pluralism in belief should not be misinterpreted as relativism or as a soft alternative to rigorous and critical thought. Pluralism in theology has always existed to some extent: Thomism, Scotism, Bonaventurianism, mysticism. It has become more evident today in view of the absence of a universally acceptable philosophy. Furthermore, a consensus exists today that a monolithic unity in the expression of faith is neither desirable nor possible. Something of the richness of Christian faith would be lost if there was absolute uniformity in the articulation of the Christian mystery. At the same time we must avoid what David Tracy calls 'a lazy pluralism within which anything can be said, since nothing, finally, is taken seriously'.[51] One remedy to this temptation is to ensure that the oneness of faith keeps together the pluralism of belief. Faith unites diversity of belief, and diversity of belief, if it is to remain religious, seeks the unity of faith.

Finally, it must be acknowledged that individuals undergo development in faith. James Fowler has mapped out different stages of faith that correspond more or less with the stages of human development.[52] These stages include:

(a) the imitative faith of the pre-school child;
(b) the literal phase of faith found in early adolescence;
(c) the synthetic stage of conventional faith in the young adult;
(d the phase of critical appropriation of faith;
(e) the phase of reworking one's faith before midlife;
(f) the phase of universal faith which is marked by inclusiveness.

The precise location and labelling of these 'stages of faith' is unimportant here. What is urgent, however, is to recognise that people undergo different stages of faith-development. This means that we must stop trying to give a child an adult (content of) faith and avoid reducing adult faith to childish proportions. Because human beings change as they grow, the appreciation of the content of faith will likewise change. The role that faith plays in the life of the individual will vary in proportion to the degree of human maturity reached. By attending to these stages of development we will be brought into contact with primordial faith that is present as universal to the human condition and its transformation into religious faith through experience. In this way the continuity and discontinuity that exist between primordial and religious faith will become more apparent. Not only that, but the importance of grounding the experience of religious Christian faith within the community, as indicated in chapter One, will also re-emerge.

The future of religious faith, therefore, lies in its relationship to and differentiation from primordial faith. In working out that relationship and differentiation closer attention will have to be given to the basic interplay that takes place between religious faith and doctrinal belief as well as the bond between the universal grace of God in the world and the personal act of faith animated by the Christian community. Most of all, the theology of faith will have to reflect more critically on the indissoluble relation that exists between God's gracious revelation in the past and in the present, which addresses every human being in experience, and to offer more imaginative interpretations of that experience through the existing wisdom of the Christian community.

QUESTIONS FOR DISCUSSION

1. Show how Christian faith only makes sense against a background of primordial faith which is shared with the rest of humanity.

2. Explain what it means to say that close relationship as well as a material difference exists between universal basic faith and particular Christian religious faith.

3. What does it mean to say that the personal act of faith addressed to the incomprehensible mystery of God is more than the content of faith contained in the Bible, early Creeds, and the teachings of the Church.

Recommended Readings
Articles
- Rahner, Karl, 'Observations on the Situation of Faith Today', *Problems and Perspectives of Fundamental Theology,* edited by René Latourelle and Gerard O'Collins, New York: Paulist Press, 1982, pp.274-291
- O'Donnell, John, 'Faith', *The New Dictionary of Theology,* edited by Joseph A. Komonchak, Mary Collins and Dermot A. Lane, Dublin: Gill and Macmillan, 1987 pp. 375-386.
- Rush, Ormond, '*Sensus Fidei:* Faith "Making Sense" of Revelation', *Theological Studies* 62 (June 2001) pp. 231-261
- Lane, Dermot A., 'Reconstructing Faith for a New Century and a New Society', *New Century, New Society: Christian Perspectives,* Edited by Dermot A. Lane, Dublin: Columba Press, 1999 pp.159-173.

Books
- Kasper, Walter, *Transcending All Understanding: The Meaning of Christian Faith Today*, San Francisco: Ignatius Press, 1987.
- Gerrish, B.A., *Saving and Secular Faith: An Invitation to Systematic Theology*, Minneapolis; Fortress Press, 1999.
- Gallagher, Michael, P., *Dive Deeper: The Human Poetry of Faith*, London: DLT, 2001

NOTES

Preface to Revised Edition

1. Gerard O'Collins, 'The Pope's Theology', *The Tablet* 27 June 1992:801.
2. An outline of this development can be found in Dermot A. Lane, *Foundations for a Social Theology: Praxis, Process and Salvation*, Dublin/New York, 1986
3. Charles Taylor, *Varieties of Religion Today: William James Revisited*, Cambridge: Harvard University Press, 2002, p.45 quoting William James from *The Will to believe, and other essays in Popular Philosophy* (1905)
4. Charles Taylor, *Varieties of Religion Today*, p.46
5. Ibid, p.47
6. Thomas M. Kelly, *Theology at the Void: The Retrieval of Experience*, Indiana: University of Notre Dame Press, 2002
7. Ibid, p.134
8. Ibid, p.136

Introduction

1. L. Gilkey, *Naming the Whirlwind* (New York: Bobbs-Merrill Company, 1969), p. 110.
2. J. Shea, *Stories of Faith* (Chicago: Thomas More Press, 1980), p. 50.
3. Ibid.

Chapter 1

1. *Karl Rahner im Gespräch, Band* 1:1964-1977, edited by Paul Imhof and Hubert Billowons (Munich: Kösel Verlag, 1982) p. 301.

2. O. Rush, *'Sensus Fidei:* Faith "Making Sense" of Revelation', *Theological Studies,* June 2001, p.236

3. D. Tracy, 'The Task of Fundamental Theology', *The Journal of Religion* 54 (1974), p.14, Tracy nuances this statement further in *Blesses Rage for Order* (New York: Seabury Press, 1975), p.43 where he points out that 'there are two sources for theology, common human experience and language, and Christian tests'.

4. M. Schmaus, *Dogma,* vol.1 (London: Sheed and Ward, 1968), p.158.

5. K. Rahner, 'Thoughts on the Possibility of Belief Today', *Theological Investigations* (hereafter as *TI*), vol. 5, (London:DLT, 1966), p.8.

6. E. Schillebeeckx, 'Faith Functioning in Human Self-Understanding', in the *Word in History* (New York: Sheed and Ward, 1966), T. P., Burke (ed.), p. 45. An elaborate account of Schillebeeckx's understanding of experience may be found in *Christ: The Christian Experience in the World* (New York: Seabury Press, 1980), pp. 30-64.

7. B. Lonergan, *Method in Theology* (London: DLT, 1972), p. 39.

8. K. Rahner, 'Theology and Anthropology', *TI*, vol.9 (1972), pp. 41-42; E. Schillebeeckx, *Understanding of the Faith* (London: Sheed and Ward, 1974), p. 17.

9. See the following random sample: Paul VI, *Mysterium Fidei*, n. 24; *Verbum Dei*, n. 14; *Gaudium et spes,* n. 10; *The General Catechetical Directory*, 1971, n. 74; John Paul II, *Catechesi Tradendae*, n. 22

10. *Redemptor hominis*, n.10.

11. P. Tillich, *Systematic Theology*, vol. 1 (Chicago: the University of Chicago Press, 1951), p. 40.

12. Ibid

13. Ibid, p. 46. There seems to be a tension in Tillich's theology about the precise role of experience. While he does state formally that experience is the medium and not the source of theology (ibid, pp. 34-53) he also gives the impression that experience can act as a source; cf. pp. 43, 46; Vol 3 (1963), pp. 221ff.

14. L. Gilkey, *Naming the Whirlwind* (New York: Bobbs-Merrill Company, 1969), p. 465.

15. Ibid., pp.316ff,253ff.

16. J. E. Smith, *Experience and God* (New York: Oxford University Press, 1968).

17. J. E. Smith, *The Analogy of Experience* (New York: Harper and Row, 1973).

18. The following account of the meaning of experience is indebted to J. E. Smith, *Experience and God*, pp. 3-45.

19. P. Winch in *The Idea of Social Science* (London: Routledge and Keegan Paul, 1953), p. 15 writes: 'Our idea of what belongs to the realm of

reality is given for us in the language that we use. The concepts we have settle for us the form of experience we have of the world.'

20. T.S. Eliot, 'Dry Salvages'.
21. G. R. Johann, 'The Return to Experience', *Review of Metaphysics* 17 (1963-1964), p. 323.
22. We are assuming here a real distinction between subjectivism, which implies loss of contact with the external world and subjectivity, which arises out of experience with reality.
23. J. Dewey, 'The Postulate of Immediate Empiricism', *Journal of Philosophy* (1907).
24. Quoted in J. Shea, *Stories of God* (Chicago: Thomas More Press, 1978), p. 16.
25. The word 'extraordinary' should not be taken to refer to sensational or unusual or exceptional or exotic or euphoric experiences. It refers primarily to that which lies both within and beyond ordinary experience.
26. See K. Rahner in K. Rahner and P. Imhof, *Ignatius of Loyola* (London: Collins, 1979), pp. 15-16.
27. P. Tillich, 'The Depth of Existence', *The Shaking of the Foundation* (London: SCM, 1949), pp. 59-70.
28. B. Lonergan, *Method in Theology*, pp. 28-31, 238-239, 263.
29. B. Lonergan, 'The Subject', *Second Collection* (London: DLT, 1974), p. 79.
39. J. E. Smith, *Experience and God*, p. 52.
31. Ibid, p. 53.
32. See for example: E.G. Bozzo, 'Theology and Religious Experience', *Theological Studies* 31(September 1970), pp.415-436; G. O'Collins, 'Theology and Experience' *Irish Theological Quarterly* 4 (1977), pp. 279-290.M.J. Buckley, 'Transcendence, Truth, and Faith: The Ascending Experience of God in all Human Inquiry', *Theological Studies* 39 December, 1978, pp. 633-655.
33. 1 Cor 13:12. Mirrors in the time of St Paul were made out of polished metal and not glass. Thus the reflection was quite indirect and obscure.
34. *Quidquid recipitur, recipitur secundum ad modum recipientis.* See ST, 1, q. 12, a. 12.
35. Rom 1:20.
36. Ex 33:20; Jn 1:18; 6:46.
37. See P. Tillich, 'Two Types of Philosophy of Religion', *Theology of Culture* (New York: Oxford, 1964), pp. 10-29, and the important critique of this article by J. C. Robertson in 'Tillich's Two Types and the Transcendental Method', *The Journal of Religion* 55 (April 1975), pp. 199-219.

38. This at times seems to be the position adopted by G. Kaufman in *An Essay on Theological Method* (Montana: Scholar's Press, 1975).
39. K. Rahner 'The Experience of God', *TI*, vol.11 (London: DLT, 1974), pp. 149-165, esp. 150-156; J. C. Robertson, art. cit., p. 216; *The Foundations of a Christian Faith* (London: DLT, 1978), pp. 51-57.
40. *ST* 1, 85, 3; 1, 86, 1: *De Verit.* 22, 2 and 1.
41. K. Rahner, *The Foundations of Christian Faith,* p. 64.
42. E. Schillebeeckx, *God and Man* (London: Sheed and Ward, 1969), p. 164.
43. J. C. Robertson, art cit., p. 316; P. Schoonenberg, 'Baptism with the Holy Spirit', *Concilium*, No 10
44. *Pensées* VII, 553.
45. T.S. Eliot, 'Little Gidding'.
46. Acts 17:28
47. K. Rahner, *The Foundations of Christian Faith*, p. 63; see also pp. 21, 34, 54, and B. Lonergan, *Method in Theology*, p. 341.
48. J. Shea, *Stories of God*, p. 33.
49. According to Rahner what is happening in mystical experience is that the traditional categorical understanding of God is being destroyed insofar as this has claimed to be ultimate. See K. Rahner 'Religious Enthusiasm and Experience of Grace', *TI, vol.* 16 (1979), p. 47.
50. See L. Gilkey, *Naming the Whirlwind* (New York: Bobbs-Merrill Company 1969), p. 296.
51. *11 Sent.Dist.* I q.I, and I; *ST* I-II q.17a 8.
52. The analogy is helpfully discussed by J. B. Bennett, 'Nature – God's Body', *Philosophy Today,* Fall 1974, pp. 248-254.
53. On the relationship between artistic experience and religious experience see R. Hazelton, *Ascending Flame, Descending Dove* (Philadelphia: Westminister, 1975), pp. 41-46.
54. This image is taken from J. C. Robertson, *art. cit,* P. 210.
55. John Paul 11, *Redemptor Hominis,* n.18
56. W. Proudfoot, 'Religious Experience, Emotion, and Belief', Harvard Theological Review July-October 1977, pp. 343-367; P. Donovan, *Intepreting Religious Experience,* pp. 28-30.
57. Traces of this restoration can be found in G. Baum, *Faith and Doctrine* (New York: Paulist Press, 1969), pp. 31-38; K. Rahner, 'Theology and Anthropology', *TI,* vol.9 (London: DLT, 1972), pp. 28-75 esp. 40-42; B. Lonergan, 'Belief: Today's Issue', *Second Collection*, pp. 87-99, esp. 88-90.
58. P. Donovan, *Interpreting Religious Experience*, pp. 66-68.
59. K. Rahner, 'The Experience of Cod', *TI,* vol.11 (London: DLT, 1974), pp. 157-158.

60. K. Rahner, *The Foundations of Christian Faith*, p. 154.
61. On this point in Rahner's theology see A. Carr, 'Theology and Experience in the Thought of K. Rahner', *The Journal of Religion* 53 (July 1973), pp. 359-376; E. Vacek 'Development within Rahner's Theology', *Irish Theological Quarterly,* XLII (January 1975), pp. 36-49; J. N. King 'The Experience of God in the Theology of K. Rahner', *Thought* 53 (July 1978), pp. 174-201.
62. K. Rahner, 'Ideology and Christianity', *TI,* vol. 6 (London: DLT, 1969), p. 51.
63. B. Lonergan, *Method in Theology*, pp. 112, 119.
64. Ibid, p. 113.
65. M. Polanyi, *Personal Knowledge* (Chicago: University of Chicago Press, 1958).
66. See E. Schillebeeckx, *The Understanding of Faith* (London: Sheed and Ward, 1974), pp. ix, 88; D. Tracy, *Blessed Rage for Order* (New York: Seabury Press, 1975), Ch. 4; S. Ogden, *The Reality of God* (New York: Harper and Row, 1963), pp. 122, 190-192; L. Gilkey, *Naming the Whirlwind*, pp. 415-426, 457ff.
67. S. Ogden, 'What Is Theology' *Journal of Religion* (January 1972); p. 25; D. Tracy, *Blessed Rage for Order*, pp. 71-72.
68. See note 67
69. S. Ogden, *The Reality of God*, pp. 6, 67, 122, 190-192; D. Tracy, *Blessed Rage for Order*, pp. 72 ff.
70. D. Tracy, *Blessed Rage for Order*, pp. 64-71.
71. E. Schillebeeckx, *The Understanding of Faith*, pp. 14-17, 20-44, 91-101.
72. D. Tracy, Blessed Rage for Order, p. 66.
73. Ibid. p. 71.
74. E. Schillebeeckx, *The Understanding of Faith*, p. 15. A similar discussion of 'meaningfulness' is found in L. Gilkey, *Naming the Whirlwind*, pp. 266-276.
75. E. Schillebeeckx, *The Understanding of Faith*, p. 17. *Naming the Whirlwind*, p. 273.
76. D. Tracy, *Blessed Rage for Order,* p. 70
77. E. Schillebeeckx, *The Understanding of Faith*, pp. 20-42.
78. D. Tracy*, Blessed Rage for Order*, pp. 67, 69.
79. Ibid., pp. 103, 135. 78. E. Schillebeeckx, *The Understanding of Faith*, pp. 91-101.
80. E. Schillebeeckx, *The Understanding of Faith*, pp. 91-101
81. John Paul II 'Faith, Science and the Search for Truth', *Origins,* 1979, p. 390.
82. See note 67.
83. Mt 7:20; see also Jas 2:17.

84. P. Tillich, *Systematic Theology,* vol. 1, pp. 43-45, 129. Tillich observes among other points: 'For those outside this situation (i.e., of revelation which requires personal participation) the same words have a different sound': ibid., p. 129. See also L. Gilkey, *Reaping the Whirlwind* (New York: Seabury Press, 1976), p. 378, n. 33.

Chapter 2

1. Michael Scanlon, 'Revelation', *The Modern Catholic Encyclopedia.* Edited by Michael Glazier and Monika K. Hellwig, Dublin: Gill and Macmillan, 747-749 at 748

2. Elizabeth Jennings, 'I Count the Moments'.

3. See G. Baum, 'Vatican II's Constitution on Revelation: History and Interpretation,' Theological Studies, March 1967, pp. 51-75; J. Ratzinger, *Commentary on the Documents of Vatican II,* H. Vorgrimler (ed.), Vol. 34 (London: Burns & Oates/Herder and Herder, 1969), pp. 155-180; G. O'Collins, *Foundations of Theology* (Chicago: Loyola University Press, 1970), Ch. 3; H. Bouillard. 'Le Concept de Revelation de Vatican I ... Vatican II,' *Revelation de Dieu et Langage des Hommes* (Paris: Editions du Cerf, 1972), pp. 35-50; N. Lash, *Change in Focus* (London: Sheed and Ward, 1973), Chts. 1 and 2.

4. A more elaborate survey of different theories of revelation is available in A. Dulles, *Revelation Theology* (London: Burns& Oates/Herder and Herder, 1969), esp. Ch. 6; 'The Problem of Revelation', *Proceedings of the Catholic Theological Society of America,* 1974, pp. 77-106; 'Symbolic Structures of Revelation', *Theological Studies,* March 1980, pp. 51-73.

5. R. Latourelle, *Theology of Revelation* (Cork: Mercier Press Ltd., 1968), esp. Ch IV; C. Moran, *Theology of Revelation* (London: Burns & Oates, 1967), esp. Ch. 1; J. Walgrave, *Unfolding Revelation* (Philadelphia: Westminister, 1972), pp. 98-99, 348ff.

6. R. Latourelle, *Theology of Revelation* (Cork: Mercier Press Ltd., 1968), esp. Ch IV; C. Moran, *Theology of Revelation* (London: Burns & Oates, 1967), esp. Ch. 1; J. Walgrave, *Unfolding Revelation* (Philadelphia: Westminister, 1972), pp. 98-99, 348ff.

7. W. Pannenberg, *Revelation as History,* p. 135.

8. J. P. Mackey, *op. cit.,* pp. 187ff.; G. O'Collins, *op. cit.,* p. 88.

9. Traces of this kind of thinking can be found in the writings of R. Bultmann. See for example Bultmann's famous essay 'New Testament and Mythology' in *Kerygma and Myth,* Vol. 1, H. Bartsch (ed.), (London: SPCK, 1964).

10. The basic principle here, namely that objectivity is the fruit of authentic subjectivity, is taken from B. Lonergan, *Method in Theology* (London: DLT, 1971), pp. 265, 292.

11. H. R. Schlette, *Epiphany as History* (London: Sheed and Ward, 1969. pp. 16ff.; J. P. Mackey, *op, cit.*, pp. 191ff; 'The Theology of Faith: A Bibliographical Survey (and More)', *New Horizons* (Fall 1975), p. 223.

12. C. Geffré, 'Esquisse d'une theologie de la Revelation,' *La Revelation,* (Bruxelles: Facult,s Universitaires St Louis, No. 7, 1977), pp. 183, 189; K. Rahner, *Foundations of Christian Faith* (London: DLT, 1978), pp. 142, 150, 152.

13. K. Rahner, *Foundations of Christian Faith* (London: DLT,1978), pp. 26-39; E. Schillebeeckx. Christ (London: SCM Press.1980), pp. 45-64. See also *Dei verbum*, n.14; John Paul II, 'Culture and Revelation', *Origins*, May 1979, pp. 15-16.

14. G. Moran, *The Present Revelation* (New York: Herder and Herder, 1972). p. 82.

15. The importance of self-consciousness is brought out effectively by W. N. Thompson in *Christ and Consciousness* (New York: Paulist Press, 1977), Cht. 8.

16. J. E. Smith, *Experience and God* (New York: Oxford University Press, 1968). p. 52.

17. W. Pannenberg, *op. cit.*, pp. 139 ff; 'The Revelation of God in Jesus of Nazareth', *New Frontiers in Theology,* Vol. 3, J. Robinson and J. B. Cobb, Jr. (eds) (New York: Harper and Row, 1967).

18. K. Rahner, 'History of the World and Salvation History', *TI,* vol.5 (London: DLT, 1966), pp. 97-114; *Foundations of Christian Faith*, pp. 142-144.

19. A useful discussion of these two extreme points of view and representative authors holding them is found in G. O'Collins, *op. cit.*, pp. 88 ff.

20. C. Geffre. *art. cit.*, p. 183

21. G. Lampe, *Christian Believing* (The Doctrine Commission of the Church of England) (London: SPCK, 1976), p. 105.

22. This particular category is foundational in the theology of J. P. Mackey. See *The Problem of Religious Faith*, (Dublin: Helicon Press, 1972), pp. 81-89, *Jesus, the Man and the Myth* (London: SCM Press, 1979), pp. 118, 135.

23. This dynamic drive toward transcendence underlies Rahner's formal theology of God. See *Foundations of Christian Faith* (London: DLT, 1978), Chts. 2 and 3. For Rahner the term of human transcendence is God: *ibid*, pp. 63-64.

24. *ST II-II, q. 2, a. 9*, and *3*. This idea is developed in detail in Chapter 3.

25. *Nostra Aetate*, n. 2. The same perspective is implicitly present in *Lumen gentium*, n. 16: *Dei verbum*, n. 3; *Gaudium et spes*, n. 22.

26. *Ad Gentes*, n.11

27. T. F. O'Meara, 'Toward a Subjective Theology of Revelation', *Theological Studies*, September 1975, p. 418: K. Rahner, *Foundations of Christian Faith*, p. 147.

28. J. Coventry, *Christian Truth* (London: DLT, 1975), p. 22

29. J. Shea, *Stories of Faith* (Chicago: Thomas More Press.1980). p. 33. See also on this point A. Dulles, 'The Problem of Revelation,' *CTSA* (1974).

30. G. Von Rad, *Old Testament Theology*, vol 1. (London: SCM Press, 1962), pp. 136 ff.

31. L. Scheffczvk, *Creation and Providence* (London: Burns & Oates, 1970), pp. 3-6.

32. C. Geffré. *art. cit.*, p. 193.

33. *Gaudium et spes*, n. 45.

34. Ibid., n. 22.

35. John Paul II, *The Pope in Ireland: Addresses and Homilies* (Dublin: Veritas, 1979). p. 47.

36. J. Ratzinger, *art. cit.*, p. 174.

37. C. Geffre, *art. cit.*, pp. 180, 190.

38. This second aspect of the uniqueness of Christian revelation is developed at length the writings of W. Pannenberg and J. Moltmann. Cf. W. Pannenberg, *Jesus – God and Man* (London: SCM Press, 1968), and J. Moltmann, *The Theology of Hope* (London: SCM Press, 1967).

39. H. Denzinger, *Enchiridion Symbolorum*, 1796-1797, 1800, 1798, 1786.

40. Ibid, 1785, 1795

41. Ibid, 1785.

42. See G. Baum, *art. cit.*; J. Ratzinger, *op. cit.;* G. O'Collins, op. cit.; H. Bouillard, *art cit.;* N. Lash, *op. cit.*

43. J. Ratzinger, *op. cit.*, p. 178.

44. This teaching of the Church (*Lamentabile* 1907) about the closure of revelation in Christ needs to be carefully interpreted if misunderstanding is to be avoided. The following points should be kept in mind.

    (a) This doctrine is as much a statement about Christology (especially concerning the finality of Christ) as it is about revelation.

    (b) This doctrine should not be taken to mean that God is no longer active in the world or that God no longer addresses God's self to the world through the experiences of humanity (deism).

    A helpful discussion of this doctrine may be found in A. Dulles, 'The Meaning of Revelation', *Theological Folia of Villanova University:*

Speculative Studies, Vol. 2, J. Papin (ed.) (Pennsylvania: Villanova University Press,1975), pp.151-179, esp. 175-178; K. Rahner, 'The Death of Jesus and the Closing of Revelation', *Theology Digest,*Winter 1975 ; W. P. Loewe, 'Dimensions and Issues,' *Living Light* (Summer 1979), esp. pp. 163-167.

45. *Gaudium et spes*, nn. 4, 11, 44.
46. The notion of experience in vogue during the modernist crisis was quite different from the one adopted in this book. Not sufficient attention was given during the modernist era to the bond between objectivity and subjectivity within human experience. Cf. note 8 above.
47. The fact that *Dei verbum* does not use the language of natural and supernatural is surely significant and marks a real contrast with Vatican I.
48. *Gaudium et spes*, n. 41; *Ad Gentes*, n. 9.

Chapter 3
1. Heinrich Fries, *Fundamental Theology,* Washington, DC: Catholic University of America Press, 1996, p. 182
2. K. Rahner, 'On the Situation of Faith', *Theological Investigations,* vol. XX, London: DLT, 1981, p. 13-14.
3. B. Lonergan, 'The Transition from a Classicist World-View to Historical Mindedness', *A Second Collection* (Philadelphia: Westminster Press, 1974).
4. R. Panikkar, 'Faith as a Constitutive Human Dimension', *Myth, Faith and Hermeneutics* (New York: Paulist Press, 1979), p. 190. This article appeared originally in *The Journal Ecumenical Studies* of (Spring 1971).
5. W. C. Smith, *Faith and Belief* (Princeton: Princeton University Press, 1979), p. 129.
6. *Ibid,* pp. 129flf.
7. R. Panikkar, *op. cit.*, p. 191.
8. James Fowler, 'Introduction', J. Fowler and R. W. Lovin (eds.) *Trajectories in Faith* (Nashville: Abingdon Press, 1980). p. 17.
9. *Ibid*, p. 19.
10. *Ibid*, pp. 19-20.
11. D. Tracy, *Blessed Rage for Order* (New York: Seabury Press, 1975), p. 8.
12. J. Wright, 'The Meaning and Structure of Catholic Faith', *Theological Studies* (December 1978), pp. 702-704.
13. J. Shea, *Stories of Faith* (Chicago: Thomas More Press, 1980), p. 44.
14. 'Preface: More Talk about Faith', *Life-Maps: Conversations on the*

Journey of Faith, by J. Fowler and S. Keen, with J. Berryman (ed.) (Texas: Word Books, 1978), p. 1.

15. Translations taken from Panikkar. op. cit., pp. 187, 220 (n. 14)

16. It is interesting to note in this regard with Panikkar that Aquinas could write that to lose faith is, in some sense, *'contra naturam'*: *ST* II-II, q. 10, a. 1 ad 1.

17. This, at times, seems to be the position taken by S. Ogden, 'The Reality of Faith', *The Reality of God and Other Essays* (New York: Harper and Row, 1963), pp. 21-43.

18. W. C. Smith, *Faith and Belief*, p. 136.

19. This section is indebted to the magisterial work of Wilfred Cantwell Smith in this area. His work, *Faith and Belief* (1979), was widely acclaimed (cf. *JES*, 1979; *RS*, 1980; *SR*, 1981).

20. W. C. Smith, *Faith and Belief*, pp. 260 (n. 30), 270 (n. 36).

21. W. C. Smith, *Belief and History* (Charlottesville: University Press of Virginia, 1977), Ch. 3.

22. W. C. Smith, *Faith and Belief*, pp. 76, 270 (n.36).

23. *ST*, II-II, q. 1, a. 2,2.

24. *ST*, II-II, q. 11, a. 1.

25. *ST*, II-II, q. 1, a. 1.

26. W. C. Smith, *Faith and Belief*, pp. 117ff.

27. W. C. Smith gives the example of a recent American dictionary which describes 'belief' as an 'opinion or conviction' and then goes on to give as an example 'the belief that the earth is flat': op. cit., p. 120.

28. *ST*, II-II, q. 1, a. 1.

29. The current emphasis in liberation theology that faith is about praxis reflects an older and more authentically Christian understanding of faith.

30. One of the basic reasons why beliefs became inflated was the predominance of a propositional view of revelation.

31. W. C. Smith, *Faith and Belief*, p. 125.

32. Cf. Panikkar, *op. cit.*, pp. 196-203.

33. See T. F. O'Meara, 'Towards a Subjective Theology of Revelation', *Theological Studies* September 1975, esp. pp. 412, 418. The universality of God's grace in the world is a major theme in the writings of K. Rahner.

34. *Gaudium et spes*: 'From the very circumstances of his origin man is already invited to converse with God' (n. 19); see also n.18 and n. 22. *Lumen gentium* points out: 'For all men are called to salvation by the grace of God' (n. 13).

35. The distinction 'first grace' and 'second grace' as found in Scripture and Christian tradition is well presented by E. Yarnold in *The Second*

Gift: A Study of Grace (Slough: St Paul Publications, 1974); cf. esp. Ch. 1.

36. *ST,* II-II, q. 1, a. 1.
37. *Super Ev. Joa.,* C. 6, lect. 5.
38. *ST, II-II,* q. 2, a. 9, and 3.
39. See J. P. Mackey, *The Problem of Religious Faith* (Dublin: Helicon Press, 1972), pp. 68-104.
40. D. Tracy, *Blessed Rage for Order,* pp. 92-109.
41. K. Rahner, *Foundations of Christian Belief* (London: DLT, 1978), pp. 26-35, 75-81.
42. K. Rahner, 'On the Significance in Redemptive History of the Individual Member of the Church', *Mission and Grace,* Vol. 1. (London: Sheed and Ward, 1963). p. 156.
43. K. Rahner, 'Anonymous and Explicit Faith', *TI,* vol.16 (London: DLT.1979), pp. 56-57.
44. W. Shea makes more or less the same point in his helpful analysis of D. Tracy in 'The Stance and Task of the Foundational Theologian', *Heythrop Journal,* October 1976, pp. 282-294.
45. *ST,* II-II, q. 1. a. 1.
46. B. Lonergan, 'Dimension of Meaning', *Collection,* F. E. Crowe (ed.) (New York: Herder and Herder, 1967), p. 266.
47. A constructive analysis of the phenomenon of indifference is offered by M. P. Gallagher in 'Towards a Pastoral Theology of Religious Indifference', *Studies* (Winter 1979).
48. Unitas Redintegratio, n. 11; The General Catechetical Directory (1971), n. 43.
49. A helpful commentary on the 'hierarchy of truths' is available in D. Carroll, 'Hierarchia Veritatum', *Irish Theological Quarter,* No. 2 (1977): U. O'Neill, 'Perspectives on the Hierarchy of Truths', *Living Light* (Summer 1979).
50. W. Kasper, *An Introduction to Christian Faith* (London: Burns & Oates, 1980), p. 104.
51. D. Tracy, 'Theological Pluralism and Analogy,' *Thought,* March 1979, p. 27.
52. A more elaborate and detailed account of the 'Stages of Faith' by Fowler can be found in *Trajectories of Faith,* pp. 21-31; *Life-Maps,* pp. 42-95.

INDEX

exterior grace, 90f; first grace, 90; second grace, 90; universal grace, 90; of God, 89

Heidegger, 21
Hierarchy of truths, 42, 95, 96
History, 27; and Christ, 63; and revelation, 48
Holy Spirit, 67, 68, 69
Hope, 62
Hopkins, G. M., 57

Imagination, 8, 11, 24, 54-56, 79
Instinct of faith, 90
Interrreligious dialogue and experience, 19
Irenaeus, 58

James, H., 23
James, W., 8, 18
Jesus, and revelation, 62f; the revelation of God, 63f; the revelation of humanity, 63; resurrection of, 62, 63
John Paul II, 18, 40
Judaism, 59f
Jung, K., 29
Justice, 62, 86

Kelly, T.M., 9, 10
Kingdom of God, 83
Kohlberg, L., 75

Language, 8, 19, 70
Lindbeck, G., 9
Linear history, 60
Liturgy, and justice, 86
Lonergan, B., 17, 24, 37, 90, 93

Mackey, J.P., 8
Meaning, 24f, 39, 40, 75
Meaningfulness, 39, 40
Modernism, 69
Monotheism, 60
Moses, 69

Mystery of God, 30, 36, 37, 66, 74
Mystical experience, 30, 31

Natural desire for God, 90
Nature and grace, 51, 89-90
New Creation, 63

O'Collins, G., 7
Ogden, S., 38
Orthodoxy, 85f
Orthopoiesis, 85f
Orthopraxis, 85f
Otto, R., 41

Pannenberg, W., 55
Panikkar, R., 75
Pascal, B., 29, 90
Paschal mystery, 42
Piaget, 75
Pius X, 17
Plato, 24
Pluralism, 74, 97
Polanyi, M., 37
Positivism, doctrinal, 43, 85
Prayer and faith, 86
Primordial faith, 76
Proofs for the existence of God, 12-13

Question of God, 12

Rahner, K., 10, 16, 17, 28, 29, 30, 37, 61, 67, 73, 83, 90, 91, 92
Rationalism, 74
Religious experience, 19, 24-33, 66f
Resurrection, 62, 63
Revelation, 46f; and faith, 51f; and history, 54f; and experience, 53; human revelation, 51f; Judaic revelation, 59f; theories of, 47f; universal revelation, 56-59
Royce, J., 41
Rush, O., 16

Sacrament, 68
Salvation, 86
Salvation history, 56
Schillebeeckx, E., 17, 28, 38-39
Schleiermacher, F. D. E., 9, 18
Schmaus, M., 17
Science, 39
Second grace, 90
Shea, J., 76
Smith, J. E., 18
Stages of faith, 97
Steiner, G., 10
Subject, and the world, 20f; intentionality of, 33
Suffering, 65
Supernatural existential, 90

Taylor, C., 8, 9
Theology, and experience, 18-19; Catholic, 17-18; fundamental, 43; Protestant, 18
Tilley, Terrence, 8
Tillich, P., 18, 30, 41, 61
Tracy, D., 8, 17, 38-39, 75, 97
Transcendence, 30
Truth, 83, 85

Understanding, and faith, 15; and experience, 21-22; pre-critical, 22; post-critical, 22
Unity, of faith, 97; between revelation and faith, 51
Unrestricted desire to know, 90

Vatican I, 66f
Vatican II, 59, 66-71, 90, 95

Word of God, 50, 53, 68
World, mediated; by meaning, 24f; immediate world, 24
Worship, 86